# Fashion Sketchbook 1920-1960

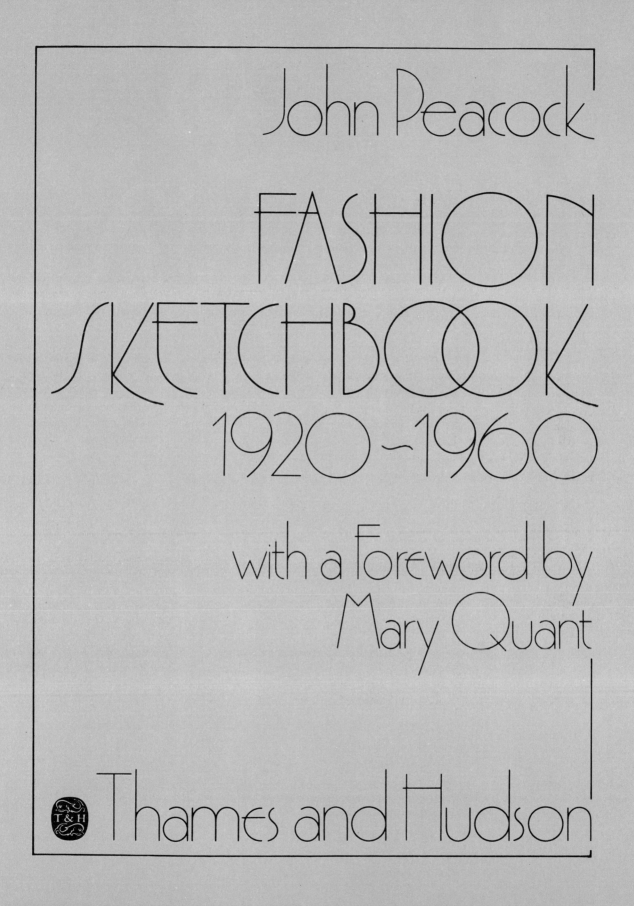

John Peacock

# FASHION SKETCHBOOK 1920-1960

with a Foreword by Mary Quant

Thames and Hudson

For my parents

*Frontispiece* (left to right):

*c.* 1926–27   Soft cotton dress with long pointed collar, sleeves cut in one with the long tubular bodice, hip-level belt, skirt with pleated centre panel. Worn with canvas hat, short gloves and 'T' strap shoes with pointed toes.

*c.* 1938–39   Crêpe dress with high yoke seams, wide padded shoulders, narrow belt at natural waist, two-tier pleated peplum matching hem detail. Worn with bow-decorated pillbox hat, long gauntlet gloves and two-tone brogue-type shoes.

*c.* 1948–50   Lilac silk dress with stiff collar, short sleeves with pointed cuffs, tight-fitting bodice to hip with tailored belt at natural waist, full skirt with wide knife-pleated panels, hem 7″ from ground. Worn with tiny bow-trimmed straw hat, short lace gloves and high-heeled slingback shoes.

*c.* 1959–60   Fine black wool dress with wide collar set on to 'V' shaped neckline, wide sleeves cut in one with loose-fitting bodice, hip belt with large bow decoration, sunray-pleated skirt over straight skirt to knee. Worn with wide straw breton hat, long gloves and stiletto-heeled shoes with pointed toes.

© 1977 Thames and Hudson Ltd, London
Reprinted 1986

Printed in Great Britain by
R. J. Acford Limited, Chichester, Sussex

# Foreword by Mary Quant

This book stops where I started, so it has the same sort of fascination for me that the novels and biographies of our parents' generation have for almost all of us.

We live in particularly nostalgic times. In recent years, fashion in the broadest sense has been flirting with the twenties and thirties, and even with the forties and fifties. It is easy to understand why the past always seems so attractive, but I think it is worth remembering that the luxuries we envy so much now were available to comparatively few people, and that many of us who enjoy this entrancing book would not have been among them.

When I started to design clothes in the mid-fifties, it was accepted that fashion was made by couturiers for princesses, film stars and the rich. Inevitably, a couple of years later, the shapes, styles and colours would percolate down to everyone else. The expected role of a designer was to translate or cheapen these ideas into what was feasible for mass production. A well-dressed woman was often a kept woman; if you had to work, you tried hard not to let it show. Gradually, with the emancipation of the sixties, it became fashionable to have a career. Even rich girls started to disguise themselves as working girls, with journalism, pop singing, fashion design, modelling or television as the best, or at any rate the most amusing, of disguises. So, for the first time, fashion came from below: stylish, sharp and disposable, to show that you earned it all yourself. Fashion was relatively cheap and co-ordinated, from head by Vidal Sassoon to toes in coloured tights.

Probably for the first time in history, it was a positive advantage to be female. It was a time of optimism, selfishness and youth, however old you were. The clothes of the early sixties anticipated this, and later indulged it. But so, too, the jeans and work-clothes of the late sixties started to anticipate the seventies, a time of general self-criticism, depression, anti-materialism and guilt. So fashion became either work-like, or nostalgic with longing for the past: it turned to the romanticized peasant, Moroccan, Chinese, Persian, Peruvian, Russian or Provençal. Today, any way to look is preferable to our own. We escape from our new problems by enjoying the old problems: cooking, gardening, needlepoint, and every other attractive craft.

Nostalgia is something that I, and probably most other fashion designers, flirt with from time to time. Reality is different: our nightmares are deadlines, workrooms without work, sheets of clean paper, architects' desks, sharp pencils and a lifetime's supply of Caran d'Ache felt-tips, expectant factories, contracts, salesmen, the dress that sold and sold and sold last year, and the American who wants to sit down and talk about it.

When I began designing, I wanted to make original fashion available to every pretty girl and to break the snobbish grip of haute couture. I admitted that Chanel invented modern clothes, and I agreed with her that many couturiers made loose covers for sofas. They seemed determined to pretend that women were some abstract shape, one season a cube, next season a tent. Chanel liked the female shape, and made clothes for women to live and work in. She made costume jewellery smart and invented style. Because of her designs, her signature scarves or bags are collectors' pieces. She made the first modern scent, aggressive and provocative, owing nothing to flowers – Chanel No. 5, the smell of tomorrow. At the end of her life, she started work on the very opposite, Chanel No. 19 – nostalgic, romantic flowers, the smell of the past.

Because of her, and because John Peacock had not produced this book, I used to spend days in the Victoria and Albert Museum, the cheapest office studio in London. Later I spent frozen afternoons under Wigmore Street in the deep storage of Debenham & Freebody, prowling through amazing Schiaparelli dresses of floor-length velvet with fur shoulders and staggering chimney-pot hats. There I developed a passionate admiration for Schiaparelli, who more or less invented boutiques, shocking pink, shoulders, outlandish sweaters, absurd hats, confidence, and Marisa Berenson.

In this book you will find four decades – twenties, thirties, forties and fifties – of dresses, sports wear, suits, coats, hats, collars, pockets, fastenings, buttons and belts, beautifully drawn with detached objectivity to amuse, inform and stimulate. Ideas will often come indirectly: I have a strange eye that transforms twenties bathing suits into fur coats, thirties knitting patterns into dresses, Romanian embroidered socks into knickers and bras, Provençal tiles into sheets and duvets, Schiaparelli hats into trousers, paint boxes and crayon tins into cosmetics, Easter eggs into scent containers, needlepoint into jacquard, and male into female or vice versa.

This book should be standard issue to all serious students of fashion. To design fashion is a subjective business: you have to start with the past to reject it, and you have to start with the past to indulge it.

London, 1976

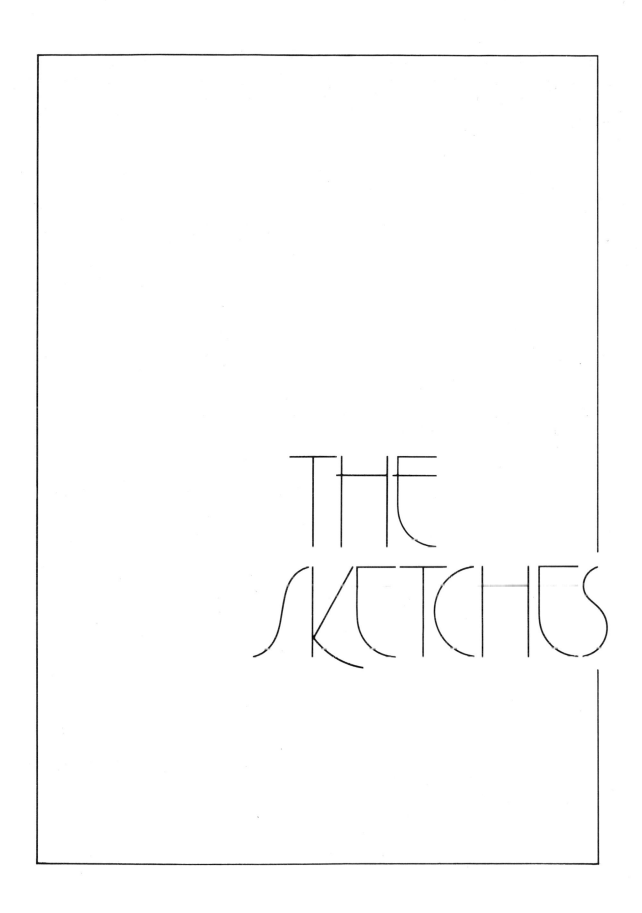

THE
SKETCHES

The Twenties 9

The Thirties 33

The Forties 65

The Fifties 97

# DAY DRESSES c.1920·22

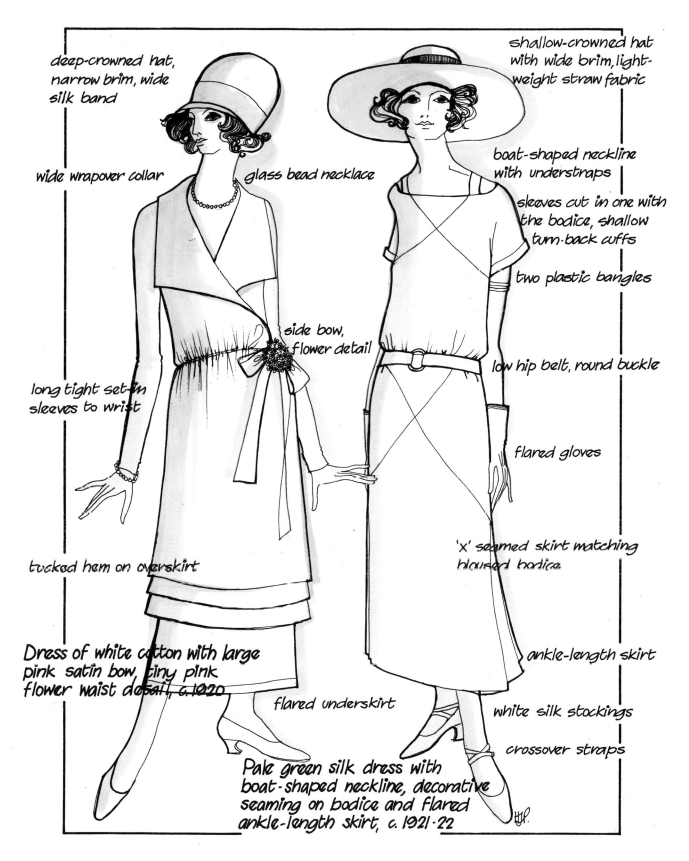

deep-crowned hat, narrow brim, wide silk band

shallow-crowned hat with wide brim, light-weight straw fabric

wide wrapover collar

glass bead necklace

boat-shaped neckline with understraps

sleeves cut in one with the bodice, shallow turn-back cuffs

two plastic bangles

side bow, flower detail

long tight set-in sleeves to wrist

low hip belt, round buckle

flared gloves

tucked hem on overskirt

'x' seamed skirt matching bloused bodice

ankle-length skirt

Dress of white cotton with large pink satin bow, tiny pink flower waist detail, c.1920

flared underskirt

white silk stockings

crossover straps

Pale green silk dress with boat-shaped neckline, decorative seaming on bodice and flared ankle-length skirt, c.1921·22

# DAY DRESSES c.1923·24

cloche hat, flower decoration at back

large stiffened organza hat

glass bead necklace

satin binding

pearl necklace

plastic cherries

cap sleeves

scarf collar

tucks

short sleeve cut in one with bodice

low hip belt

bishop sleeves, tucked cuffs

Lace dress over satin slip with low satin hip belt and bows, c.1924

pleated side panels

satin shoes

Blue silk mid-calf-length dress, striped scarf collar and half-belt, c.1923

blue kid shoes with white inset scallops

Wool and silk dress with two low-placed tailored belts, c.1924

soft leather shoes, high louis heel

# DAY DRESSES c.1925·26

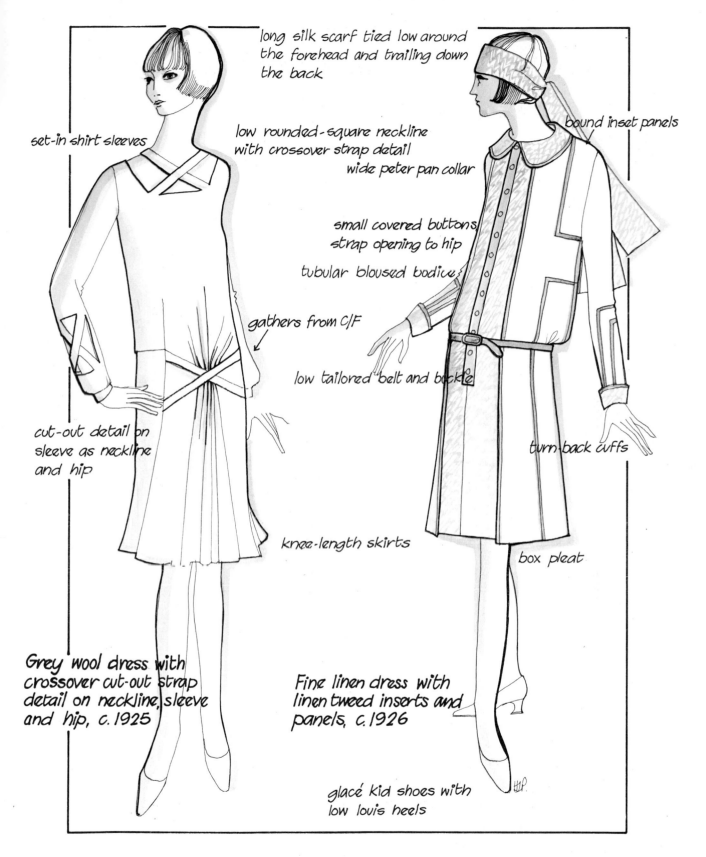

long silk scarf tied low around the forehead and trailing down the back

set-in shirt sleeves

low rounded-square neckline with crossover strap detail

wide peter pan collar

bound inset panels

small covered buttons, strap opening to hip

tubular bloused bodice

gathers from C/F

cut-out detail on sleeve as neckline and hip

low tailored belt and buckle

turn-back cuffs

knee-length skirts

box pleat

Grey wool dress with crossover cut-out strap detail on neckline, sleeve and hip, c.1925

Fine linen dress with linen tweed inserts and panels, c.1926

glacé kid shoes with low louis heels

# DAY DRESSES c.1927·29

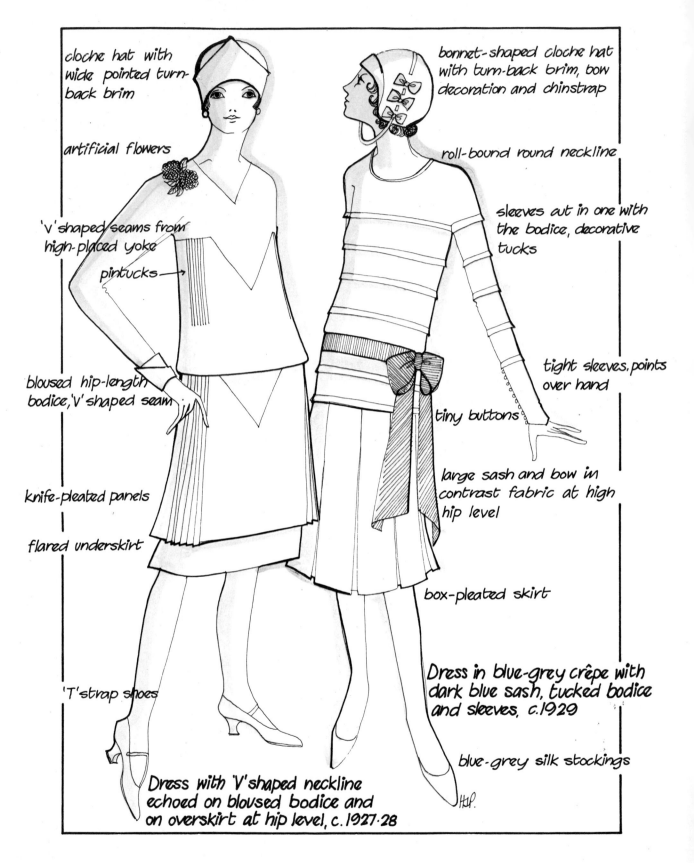

cloche hat with wide pointed turn-back brim

bonnet-shaped cloche hat with turn-back brim, bow decoration and chinstrap

artificial flowers

roll-bound round neckline

'v'shaped seams from high-placed yoke

sleeves cut in one with the bodice, decorative tucks

pintucks

bl.oused hip-length bodice,'v'shaped seam

tight sleeves, points over hand

tiny buttons

knife-pleated panels

large sash and bow in contrast fabric at high hip level

flared underskirt

box-pleated skirt

'T'strap shoes

Dress in blue-grey crêpe with dark blue sash, tucked bodice and sleeves, c.1929

blue-grey silk stockings

Dress with 'V'shaped neckline echoed on bloused bodice and on overskirt at hip level, c.1927·28

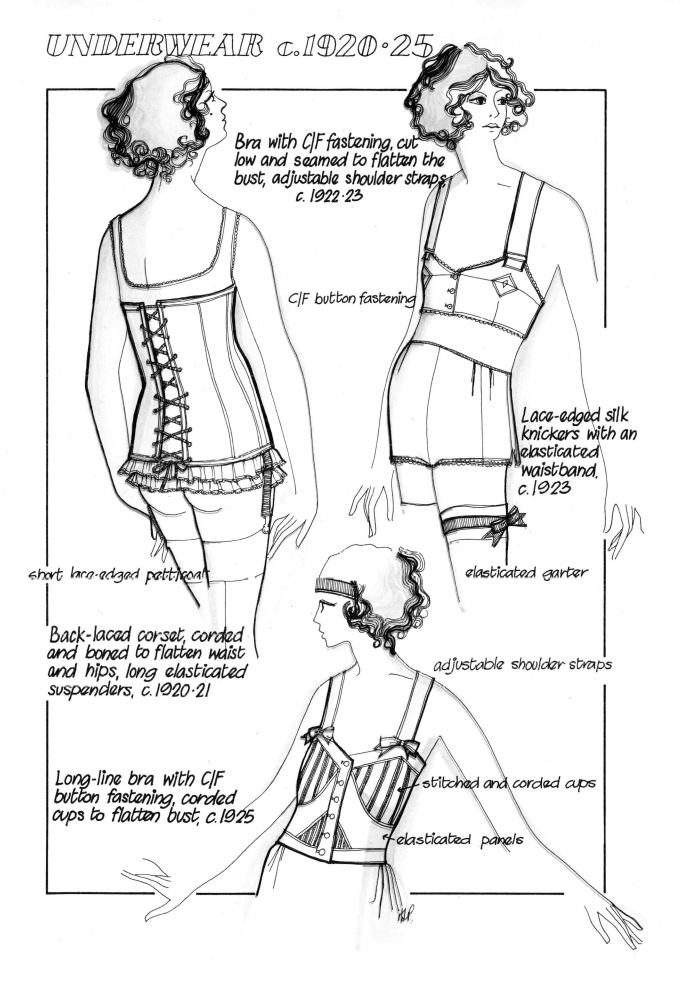

Bra with C/F fastening, cut low and seamed to flatten the bust, adjustable shoulder straps. c.1922·23

C/F button fastening

Lace-edged silk knickers with an elasticated waistband. c.1923

elasticated garter

short lace-edged petticoat

Back-laced corset, corded and boned to flatten waist and hips, long elasticated suspenders, c.1920·21

adjustable shoulder straps

Long-line bra with C/F button fastening, corded cups to flatten bust, c.1925

stitched and corded cups

elasticated panels

bust-flattener bra,
buttoned straps

elasticated panels

Fully elasticated
bra, girdle and
suspenders, joined
at waist with
straps, c.1925

Corset with elasticated panels
and suspenders, lace edging,
c.1925

Corset with elasticated
front panel, worn over
a short lace-edged
petticoat, c.1928·29

Soft bra, cut low and
seamed to give a smooth
rounded bustline, c.1929

Brocade corset, corded and
stitched over bust to waist,
elasticated panels set in
over hips, c.1926

Tubular petticoat with narrow shoulder straps, horizontal tucks with lace inserts at neck, hip and hemline, pintucks either side of bust through to hem, c.1926·27

narrow shoulder straps, low round neckline with lace inserts

low waistline

scalloped hemline, lace edge, rouleau bow detail

Pure silk petticoat with fine lace inserts and satin trim, c. 1926

velvet slippers with satin flower trim

Silk petticoat with pouched bodice, fine silk flower embroidery, straps, neckline and hemline of embroidered braid, c.1928·29

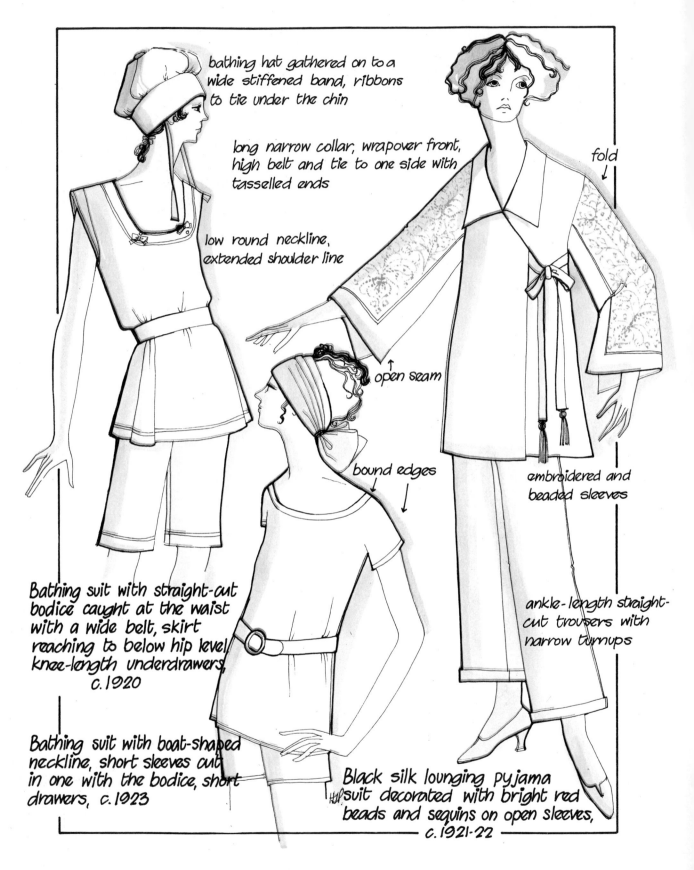

bathing hat gathered on to a wide stiffened band, ribbons to tie under the chin

long narrow collar, wrapover front, high belt and tie to one side with tasselled ends

fold

low round neckline, extended shoulder line

open seam

bound edges

embroidered and beaded sleeves

Bathing suit with straight-cut bodice caught at the waist with a wide belt, skirt reaching to below hip level, knee-length underdrawers, c.1920

ankle-length straight-cut trousers with narrow turnups

Bathing suit with boat-shaped neckline, short sleeves cut in one with the bodice, short drawers, c.1923

Black silk lounging pyjama suit decorated with bright red beads and sequins on open sleeves, c.1921-22

# LEISURE WEAR c.1924·25

headband with strap decoration

square neckline, button-down straps

long tubular bodice

button and strap detail

accordion-pleated skirt

white straw cloche hat with slightly flared brim and narrow coloured band

braided collar, matching sleeves cut in one with bodice, turn-back cuffs

loop and button fastening

long bloused bodice

low hip belt with decorative threaded covered buckle

flared skirt to just below knee

Tennis dress in white cotton, sleeveless, with square strap-decorated neckline, matching hip detail, c.1924·25

white canvas tennis shoes

Tennis dress with long bloused bodice, braided hip belt, matching collar, sleeves and hat, flared skirt, c.1925

cotton ankle socks, soft canvas shoes

# LEISURE WEAR c.1926·29

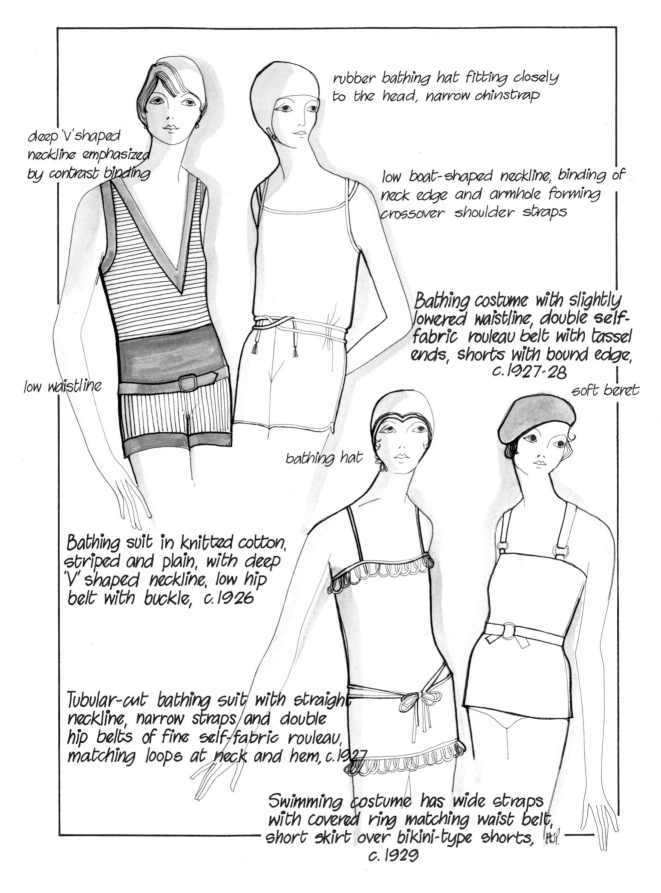

deep 'V' shaped neckline emphasized by contrast binding

rubber bathing hat fitting closely to the head, narrow chinstrap

low boat-shaped neckline, binding of neck edge and armhole forming crossover shoulder straps

Bathing costume with slightly lowered waistline, double self-fabric rouleau belt with tassel ends, shorts with bound edge, c.1927-28

soft beret

low waistline

bathing hat

Bathing suit in knitted cotton, striped and plain, with deep 'V' shaped neckline, low hip belt with buckle, c.1926

Tubular-cut bathing suit with straight neckline, narrow straps and double hip belts of fine self-fabric rouleau, matching loops at neck and hem, c.1927

Swimming costume has wide straps with covered ring matching waist belt, short skirt over bikini-type shorts, c.1929

# EVENING DRESSES c. 1920·24

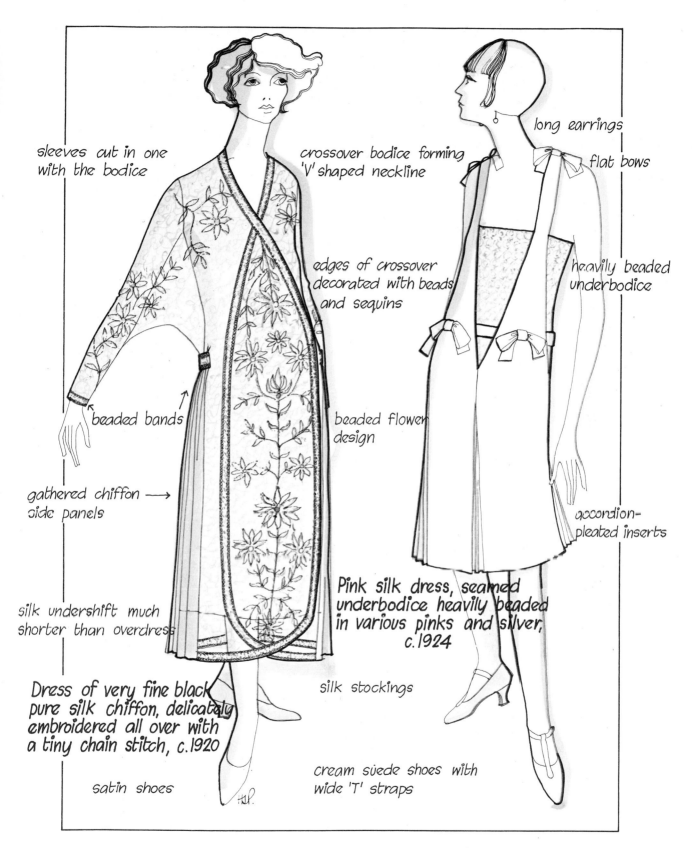

sleeves cut in one
with the bodice

crossover bodice forming
'V' shaped neckline

long earrings

flat bows

edges of crossover
decorated with beads
and sequins

heavily beaded
underbodice

beaded bands

beaded flower
design

gathered chiffon
side panels

accordion-
pleated inserts

Pink silk dress, seamed
underbodice heavily beaded
in various pinks and silver,
c.1924

silk undershift much
shorter than overdress

Dress of very fine black
pure silk chiffon, delicately
embroidered all over with
a tiny chain stitch, c.1920

silk stockings

satin shoes

cream suede shoes with
wide 'T' straps

# EVENING DRESSES c.1925·26

low boat-shaped neckline bound with sequins

low 'U' shaped neckline with flesh-coloured insert, large silk flower worn high on one shoulder

black sequined vest insert

bias-cut collar

bead design on wrapover bodice

three-tier skirt

hemline dipping either side

Dress with long tubular bodice to very low waist decorated with geometric design of brightly coloured sequins, gathered two-tier skirt to just below knee, c.1925

↑
Dress of pale orange crêpe with bands of plastic sequins in a deeper orange, c.1926

Coat-style dress of grey silk crêpe, sequined vest, gathered three-tier skirt, c.1926

silver kid shoes, high louis heels

# EVENING DRESSES c. 1927·29

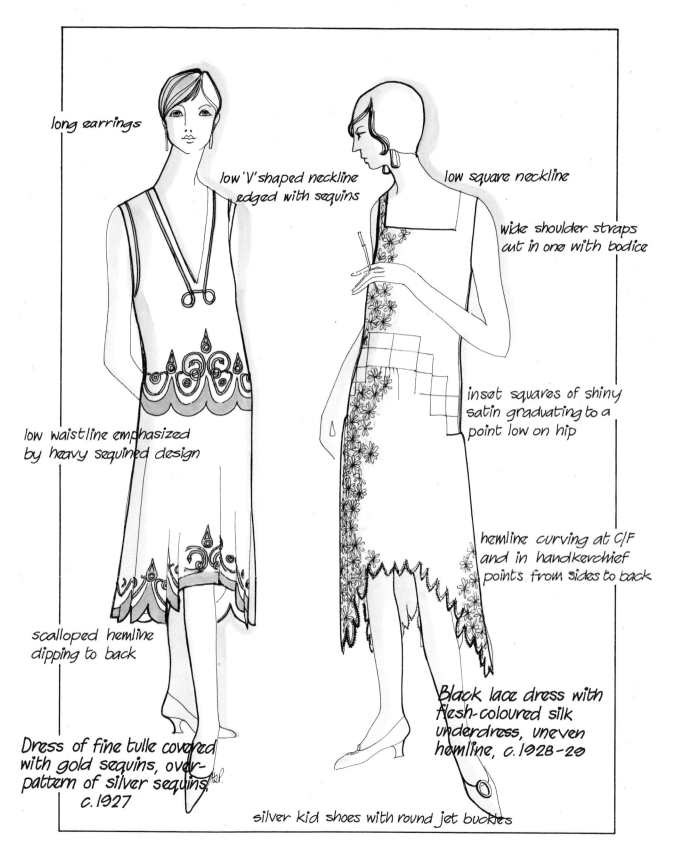

long earrings

low 'V' shaped neckline
edged with sequins

low square neckline

wide shoulder straps
cut in one with bodice

low waistline emphasized
by heavy sequined design

inset squares of shiny
satin graduating to a
point low on hip

hemline curving at C/F
and in handkerchief
points from sides to back

scalloped hemline
dipping to back

Black lace dress with
flesh-coloured silk
underdress, uneven
hemline, c. 1928-29

Dress of fine tulle covered
with gold sequins, over-
pattern of silver sequins,
c. 1927

silver kid shoes with round jet buckles

# WEDDING DRESSES c.1920·25

tall turban banded with pearls and trimmed with tiny flowers

hat with tall crown, wide brim

tucks

short set-in sleeves

honeycomb-stitched part

long kid gloves

fine chiffon veil with delicate embroidered edge

low 'U' shaped neckline

shirt-type sleeves, flared lace oversleeves

ankle-length gathered skirt

Dress with tubular-shaped bodice to low waist, gathered skirt to just below knee, lace overdress, c.1924-25

Cream silk dress with short sleeves, natural waistline emphasized by narrow belt and two flat bows, c.1920-22

soft kid shoes, strap over the instep, cut-out design

# WEDDING DRESSES c.1926·29

large hat with brim turned back to one side

deep cloche hat

artificial flowers

low necklines

long tight sleeves

button-down strap decoration

bloused bodices

wrapover bodice to low-waist

draped basque

wide bishop-type sleeves

Dress in dark cream crêpe, low waist detail, skirt with rounded floating panels over a knife-pleated underskirt. c.1926-27

Pale lilac silk dress worn with grey accessories, c.1929

overskirt with handkerchief points over gathered skirt

pale grey silk stockings

fine leather shoes with punched hole decoration

pointed shoes, fine materials

# SUITS c.1920·22

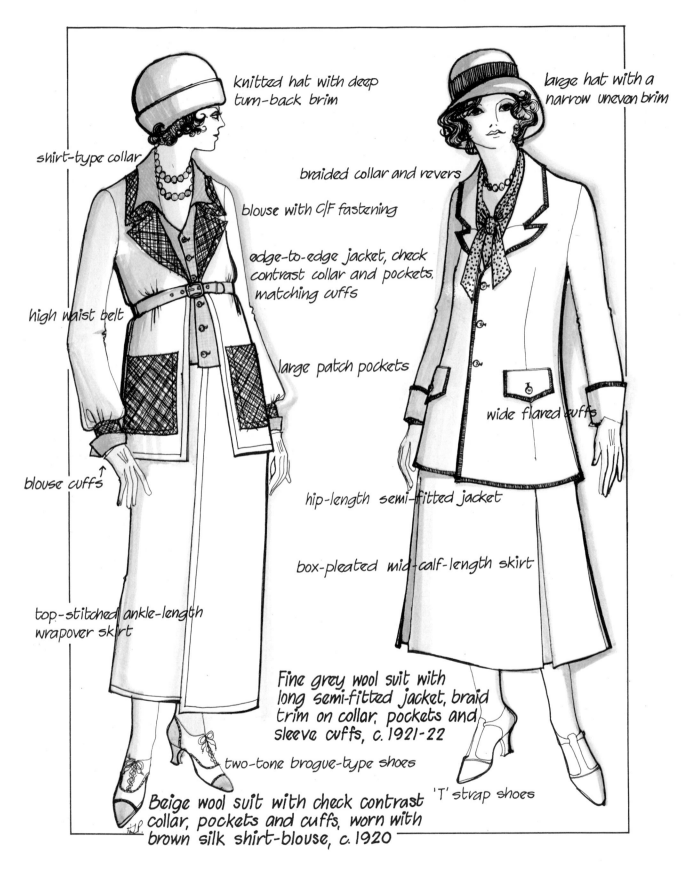

knitted hat with deep turn-back brim

large hat with a narrow uneven brim

shirt-type collar

braided collar and revers

blouse with C/F fastening

edge-to-edge jacket, check contrast collar and pockets, matching cuffs

high waist belt

large patch pockets

wide flared cuffs

blouse cuffs

hip-length semi-fitted jacket

box-pleated mid-calf-length skirt

top-stitched ankle-length wrapover skirt

Fine grey wool suit with long semi-fitted jacket, braid trim on collar, pockets and sleeve cuffs, c.1921-22

two-tone brogue-type shoes

Beige wool suit with check contrast collar, pockets and cuffs, worn with brown silk shirt-blouse, c.1920

'T' strap shoes

# SUITS c. 1923·24

hard felt hat with turn-back brim, deep band, feather trim

round neckline with bound contrast facing

contrast cuff

low bound contrast hip belt, round buckle

C/F false strap opening in contrast fabric

mid-calf-length skirt, plain centre panel with knife pleats on either side

Cream linen suit with navy blue linen contrast straps and buttons, c.1923

pointed toes

straw cloche, false brim turned back and covered with lace to match trailing ends, side feather decoration

lace-edged modesty vest

jacket open to bustline, lace strap decoration

C/F loop and button fastening

sleeve cut in one with bodice and gathered into a lace cuff

mid-calf-length skirt with knife-pleated front panel

Pale blue crêpe suit with cream lace decoration, c.1924

double shoe straps

# SUITS c. 1925·26

cloche hat with tiny turn-back brim at front, side flower and bow trim

straw hat with narrow turn-down brim, worn to one side of head

fox-fur collar, matching cuffs

mock shirt-blouse, stiff bow tie

striped waistcoat

long straight-cut jacket, contrast collar and bindings

hip belt

stiff shirt cuffs, cufflinks

low tie belt

narrow contrast welt pockets

knee-length box-pleated skirt

tiny pleated inserted panels

Suit in yellow wool trimmed with black collar, pockets, belt and bindings, c. 1926

Orange wool crêpe suit with cream bindings, fox-fur collar and cuffs, worn with cream and orange striped waistcoat, c.1925

two-tone shoes with high louis heels and pointed toes

pointed shoes with tiny bow trim

# SUITS c. 1927·29

hat with wide brim bound
with spotted silk, large
bow with fringed ends

spotted silk tie

underblouse buttoned
through to waist

tucks

horizontal tucks repeated
in flared skirt

Suit in pale green linen with
darker green and white spotted
contrast trimmings. c. 1927-28

fine leather shoes with
strap over instep

cloche hat in straw
with contrast-colour brim

bunch of artificial
violets
high yoke with gathers

blouse in contrast fabric
with deep 'V' shaped neckline bound with main
body fabric

bound 'V' shaped pockets

tight sleeves with
flared bound cuffs

flared skirt with contrast
'V' shaped insert

Suit in fine wool crêpe
with blouse and contrast
inserts in a dark-coloured
satin, c. 1928-29

# COATS c.1920·23

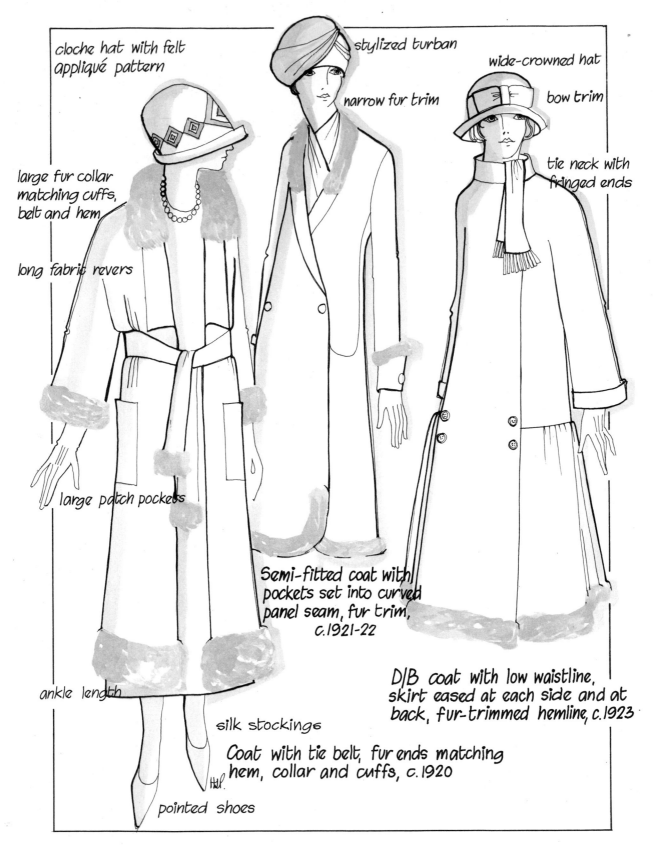

cloche hat with felt appliqué pattern

stylized turban

wide-crowned hat

narrow fur trim

bow trim

large fur collar matching cuffs, belt and hem

tie neck with fringed ends

long fabric revers

large patch pockets

Semi-fitted coat with pockets set into curved panel seam, fur trim, c.1921-22

D/B coat with low waistline, skirt eased at each side and at back, fur-trimmed hemline, c.1923

ankle length

silk stockings

Coat with tie belt, fur ends matching hem, collar and cuffs, c.1920

pointed shoes

# COATS c.1924·26

trilby-type hat

cloche hat, side bow detail

soft hat, wide brim, felt flower trim

fur collar matching wide cuffs

fur attached to shawl collar

fur cuffs

hip seam

flap pockets

side button fastening

diagonally striped skirt

knee length

Slim-fitting coat with thick bands of fur at the neck, cuffs and hem, c.1925-26

Dark brown tweed coat, wrapover front, diagonally striped tweed skirt, fox-fur trimming on collar and cuffs, c.1924

Tweed coat, wrapover to one side, two-button fastening, sleeve with wide hem flare and tiny button trim, c.1925

29

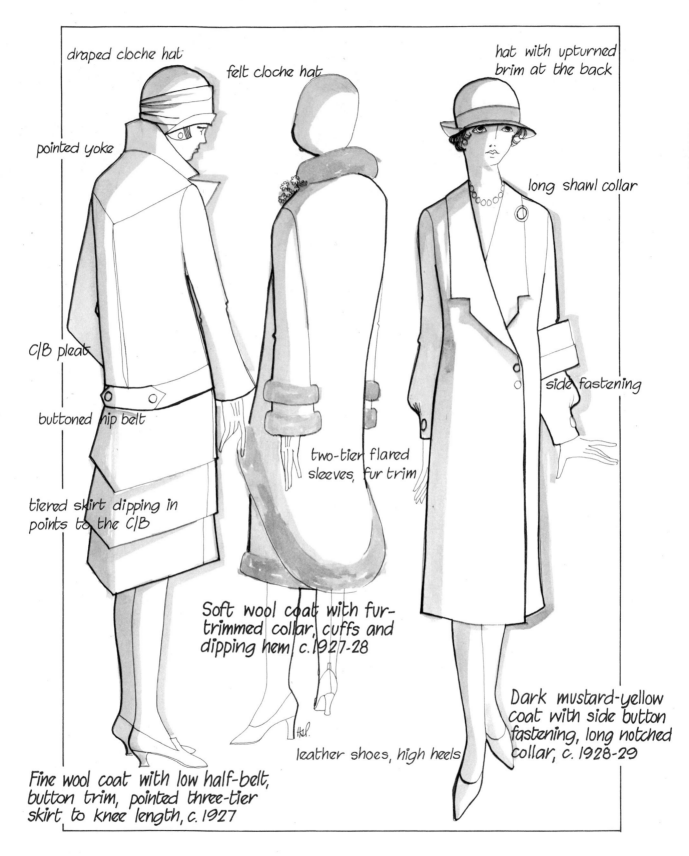

draped cloche hat

felt cloche hat

hat with upturned brim at the back

pointed yoke

long shawl collar

C/B pleat

buttoned hip belt

side fastening

tiered skirt dipping in points to the C/B

two-tier flared sleeves, fur trim

Soft wool coat with fur-trimmed collar, cuffs and dipping hem, c.1927-28

leather shoes, high heels

Dark mustard-yellow coat with side button fastening, long notched collar, c. 1928-29

Fine wool coat with low half-belt, button trim, pointed three-tier skirt to knee length, c. 1927

flowerpot hat trimmed with fine pleated organza, c.1920-21

wide-brimmed lace hat trimmed with satin and flowers, c.1920

straw hat with velvet band and bow, c.1923

scarf and plastic ring, c.1920-22

scarf with embroidered initials, c.1923-24

cloche hat with scalloped upturned brim, side feather trim, c. 1924-26

large hat with split brim, c.1927

cloche hat, long silk tie, c.1928

purse, c.1929

diamanté bow brooch

scalloped gloves

long beads

hat with plaited band detail c.1927

evening turban, c.1927

envelope purse

envelope purse with ribbon handle, c.1926

gauntlet gloves, c.1927-28

feather and bead evening purse, c.1927

cloche hat, narrow turn-back brim, feather trim to one side, c.1928

felt hat with wide upturned brim, c.1928

tall stiff straw cloche, split brim, c.1927

felt flowers

long graduated glass bead necklace

long suede gloves

shawl with fringed hem, c.1927-28

cloche hat with stitched braid trim, c.1929

'T' strap shoes, c.1928

fine kid, single strap, c.1923-24

leather shoes with 'X' strap, c.1925

two-tone leather, c.1924-25

silk evening bag, c.1926

fur scarf, c.1929

¾ length gloves

leather handbag with long handle, c.1927-28

suede inserts, c.1927

two straps, punched hole pattern, c.1927-28

high heel, ankle strap, c.1929

velvet house mules, c.1926

# DAY DRESSES c.1930·32

soft felt hat with bow trim

wide contrast bindings

peter pan collar

straw hat with pointed crown, buckle trim

contrast bindings

tucks

strap decoration at the neck, waist and cuff

tight set-in sleeves, false cuff above binding

narrow box pleats

Yellow wool dress and jacket with black binding, straight-cut jacket, skirt with gentle flare and side pleats from the waist, c.1932

D/B grey linen dress with decorative binding in dark red linen, c.1930

Navy blue wool dress with side button fastening, wide belt, decorative buckle, c.1931

cream silk stockings

snakeskin shoes with leather trim

soft leather shoes with high heels and single strap

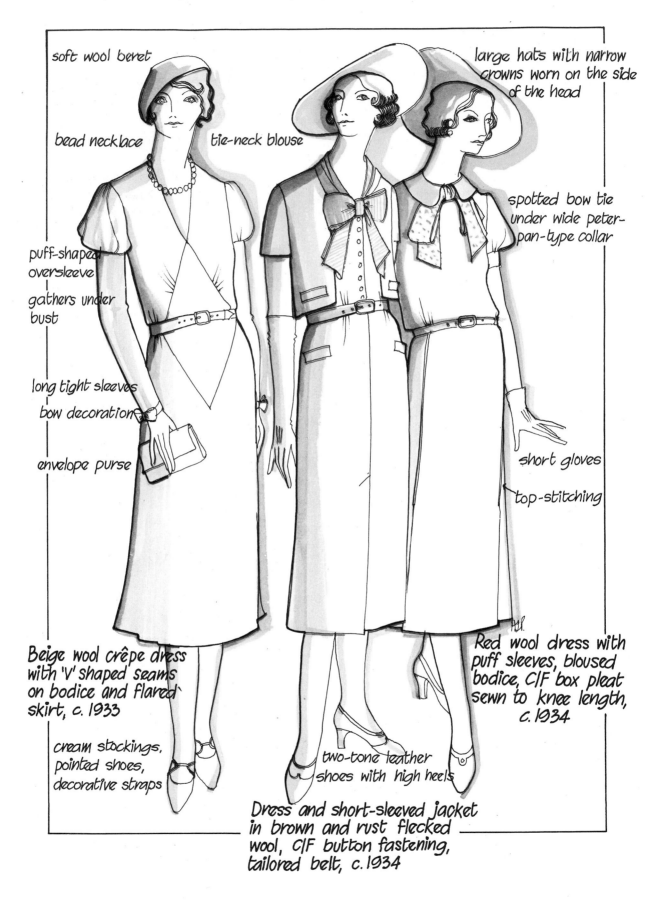

# DAY DRESSES c. 1933·34

soft wool beret

large hats with narrow crowns worn on the side of the head

bead necklace

tie-neck blouse

puff-shaped oversleeve

spotted bow tie under wide peter-pan-type collar

gathers under bust

long tight sleeves

bow decoration

envelope purse

short gloves

top-stitching

Beige wool crêpe dress with 'V' shaped seams on bodice and flared skirt, c. 1933

Red wool dress with puff sleeves, bloused bodice, C/F box pleat sewn to knee length, c. 1934

cream stockings, pointed shoes, decorative straps

two-tone leather shoes with high heels

Dress and short-sleeved jacket in brown and rust flecked wool, C/F button fastening, tailored belt, c. 1934

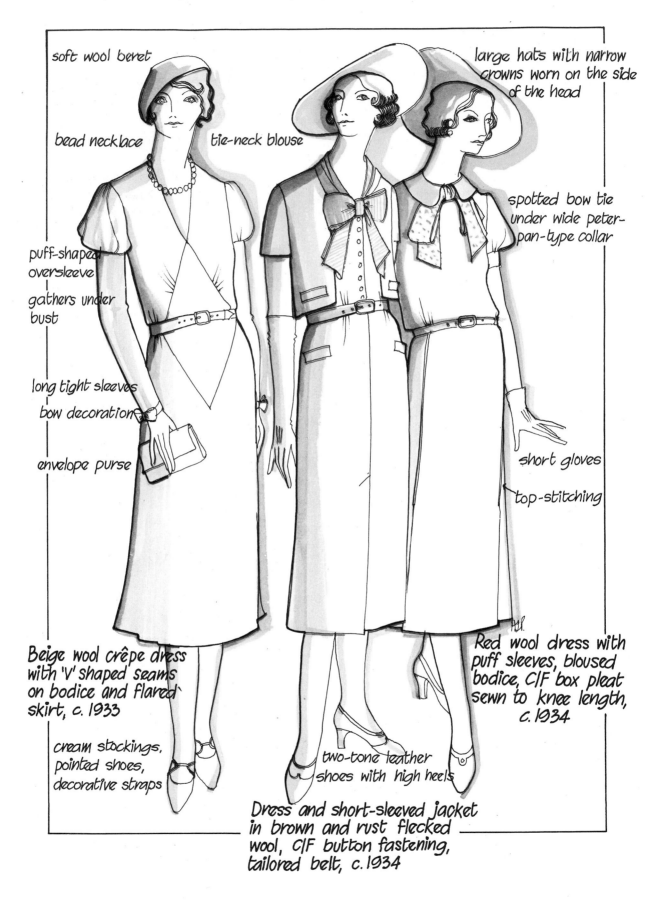

34

# DAY DRESSES c. 1933·36

fine straw hat with wide crown and narrow brim, braid trim

deep eton-type collar

welt pockets, button trim

wide leather belt

buttoned cuff

knife pleats sewn to knee length

Plum-coloured tailored dress with long tight sleeves, slightly bloused bodice and a gently flared skirt with side pleats, c. 1933

fine leather shoes with C/F seam

flat straw hat trimmed with bows and flowers

bow tie under flat collar

short set-in sleeves with gathered head and narrow turn-back cuffs

patch pockets

belt with bow decoration

short gloves flared at wrist

inverted box pleat

mid-calf-length skirt

Dress in dark green wool with white trimming and a C/F box pleat from neckline to hem, c. 1936

snakeskin court shoes with high heels and pointed toes

fabric hair slide to match dress

large berthe collar in white cotton piqué

fine lace edging

wide belt with round black plastic buckle

white cotton piqué turn-back cuffs with lace edging

peter pan collar with frilled edging, pockets and cuffs to match

short puff sleeves with cuff

tiny welt pocket

covered buttons

narrow tailored belt, self-fabric-covered buckle

gathered patch pockets

Dress in turquoise wool georgette with button-through fastening to waist, full skirt to knee length, c. 1939

nylon stockings

Button-through dress in mustard-coloured wool with white collar and cuffs, flared skirt with C/F inverted box pleat, c. 1937

suede court shoes with elongated toes

leather court shoes, almond-shaped toes, high thick heels

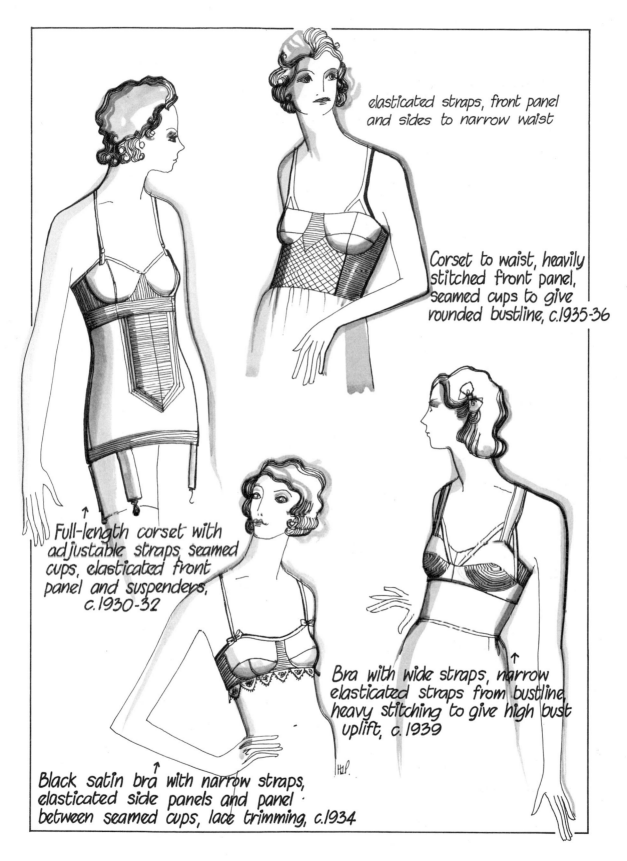

elasticated straps, front panel and sides to narrow waist

Corset to waist, heavily stitched front panel, seamed cups to give rounded bustline, c.1935-36

Full-length corset with adjustable straps seamed cups, elasticated front panel and suspenders, c.1930-32

Bra with wide straps, narrow elasticated straps from bustline, heavy stitching to give high bust uplift, c.1939

Black satin bra with narrow straps, elasticated side panels and panel between seamed cups, lace trimming, c.1934

square neckline, narrow straps

diamond-shaped seam, tie belt

back view showing scooped-out neckline

Petticoat with double straps, appliqué lace decoration round low scalloped neckline and hem. c. 1930·32

Short black satin petticoat with rouleau tie belt at waist, decorative seaming, gathers under bust, c. 1937

velvet house slippers trimmed with feathers

Dark green cami-knickers with wide shoulder straps and bindings in black satin, large appliqué embroidered leaves, c. 1939

Silk petticoat with gathered waist seam, delicate embroidery at neck and hem, c. 1932

hat with deep crown, down-turned brim with flower decoration

low 'U' shaped neckline

artificial flowers

tucked bodice

fur cuffs

long tight sleeves with point over hand

two-tier knife-pleated skirt

ankle length

Dress and jacket in pale grey-blue wool georgette, c.1933

grey leather shoes with low heel

large-brimmed hat with shallow flat crown

two rows of double silk organza frills

long kid gloves

bloused bodice

wide belt, large bow tie

double frill at hip level

flared skirt

Pale lilac silk and silk organza full-length dress worn to garden parties and race meetings, c.1934

pale lilac kid shoes with narrow diagonal strap and bow decoration

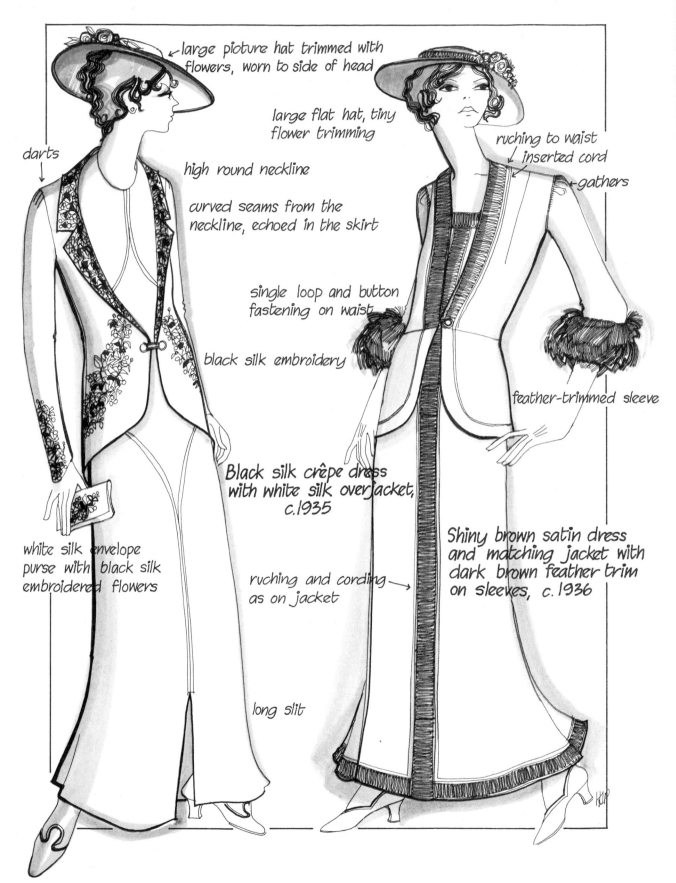

large picture hat trimmed with flowers, worn to side of head

large flat hat, tiny flower trimming

high round neckline

curved seams from the neckline, echoed in the skirt

single loop and button fastening on waist

black silk embroidery

darts

ruching to waist

inserted cord

gathers

feather-trimmed sleeve

Black silk crêpe dress with white silk overjacket, c.1935

white silk envelope purse with black silk embroidered flowers

ruching and cording as on jacket

long slit

Shiny brown satin dress and matching jacket with dark brown feather trim on sleeves, c.1936

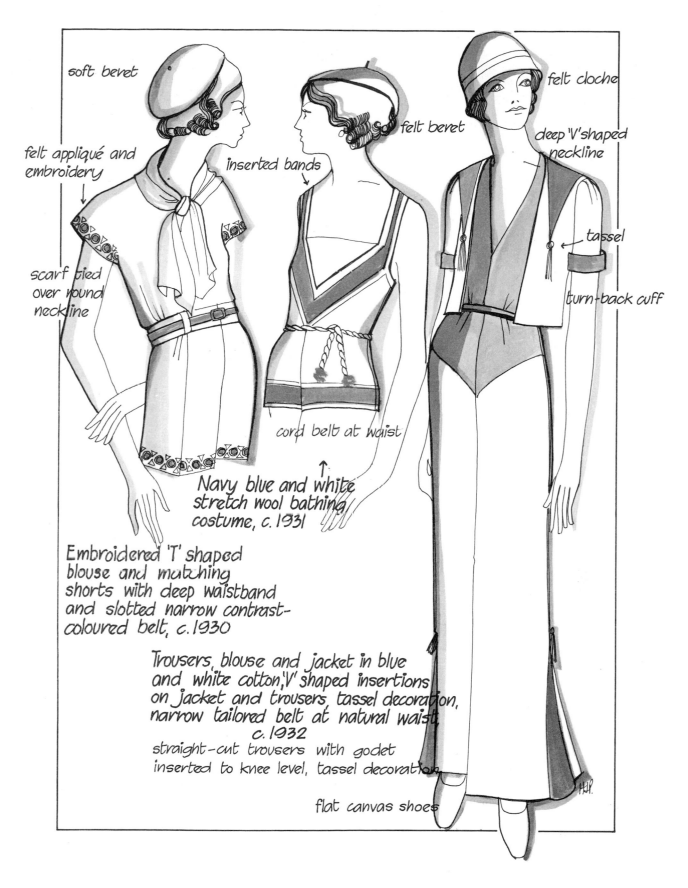

soft beret

felt cloche

felt appliqué and embroidery

felt beret

deep 'V'shaped neckline

inserted bands

scarf tied over round neckline

tassel

turn-back cuff

cord belt at waist

Navy blue and white stretch wool bathing costume, c.1931

Embroidered 'T' shaped blouse and matching shorts with deep waistband and slotted narrow contrast-coloured belt, c.1930

Trousers, blouse and jacket in blue and white cotton,'V' shaped insertions on jacket and trousers, tassel decoration, narrow tailored belt at natural waist. c.1932
straight-cut trousers with godet inserted to knee level, tassel decoration

flat canvas shoes

# LEISURE WEAR c. 1933·34

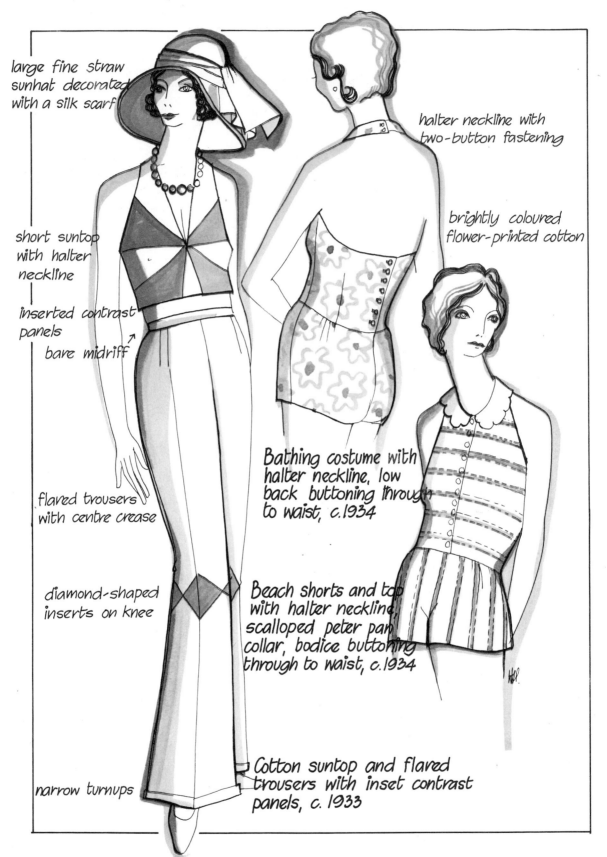

large fine straw sunhat decorated with a silk scarf

halter neckline with two-button fastening

short suntop with halter neckline

brightly coloured flower-printed cotton

inserted contrast panels

bare midriff

flared trousers with centre crease

Bathing costume with halter neckline, low back buttoning through to waist, c.1934

diamond-shaped inserts on knee

Beach shorts and top with halter neckline, scalloped peter pan collar, bodice buttoning through to waist, c.1934

narrow turnups

Cotton suntop and flared trousers with inset contrast panels, c. 1933

# LEISURE WEAR c.1935·36

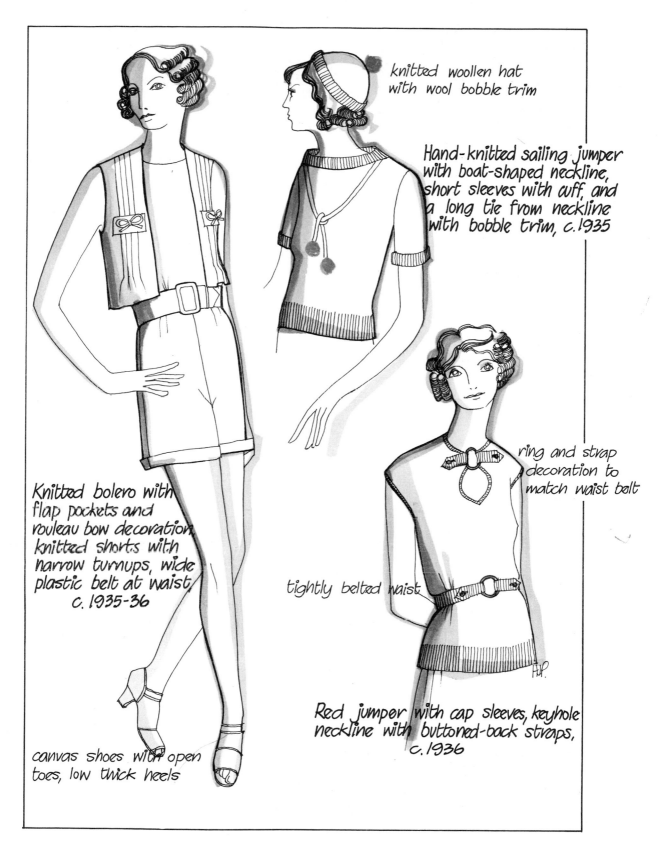

knitted woollen hat
with wool bobble trim

Hand-knitted sailing jumper
with boat-shaped neckline,
short sleeves with cuff, and
a long tie from neckline
with bobble trim, c.1935

Knitted bolero with
flap pockets and
rouleau bow decoration,
knitted shorts with
narrow turnups, wide
plastic belt at waist,
c.1935-36

canvas shoes with open
toes, low thick heels

ring and strap
decoration to
match waist belt

tightly belted waist

Red jumper with cap sleeves, keyhole
neckline with buttoned-back straps,
c.1936

plastic choker and matching earring

straw beret with braid trimming

tucked sleeve head

wide bound collar

braid decoration

twisted loop and covered button fastening

slightly flared 3/4 length sleeves

sleeve binding and blouse in matching fabric

wide trousers with centre crease

Red wool trouser suit with edge-to-edge loop and button fastening, 3/4 length sleeves and black braid trimming, c.1937

Trouser suit in white linen with green and white spotted silk binding, blouse and waist sash, c.1939

wide flared trousers

wide turnups

crossed-strap sandals, thick platform soles

strap sandals with thin platform

long beads

square neckline

applied lace →
overbodice

tiny tucks

long tight sleeves

gathered skirt

deep gathered frill

narrow shoulder straps

low neckline

large silk flowers

long satin evening gloves

complicated cross-seaming

Long cream satin evening dress with bias-cut bodice to low hip level and circular-cut skirt, c. 1931-32

satin shoes with elongated toes

Black lace and organza dress with pink silk underdress, c. 1930

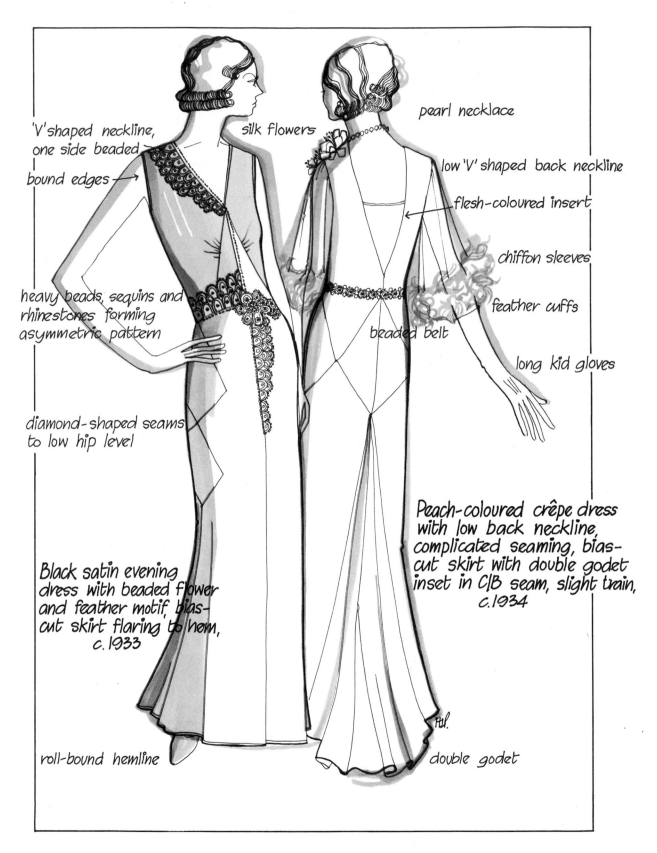

'V' shaped neckline, one side beaded

bound edges

silk flowers

pearl necklace

low 'V' shaped back neckline

flesh-coloured insert

chiffon sleeves

heavy beads, sequins and rhinestones forming asymmetric pattern

feather cuffs

beaded belt

long kid gloves

diamond-shaped seams to low hip level

Black satin evening dress with beaded flower and feather motif, bias-cut skirt flaring to hem, c.1933

Peach-coloured crêpe dress with low back neckline, complicated seaming, bias-cut skirt with double godet inset in C/B seam, slight train, c.1934

roll-bound hemline

double godet

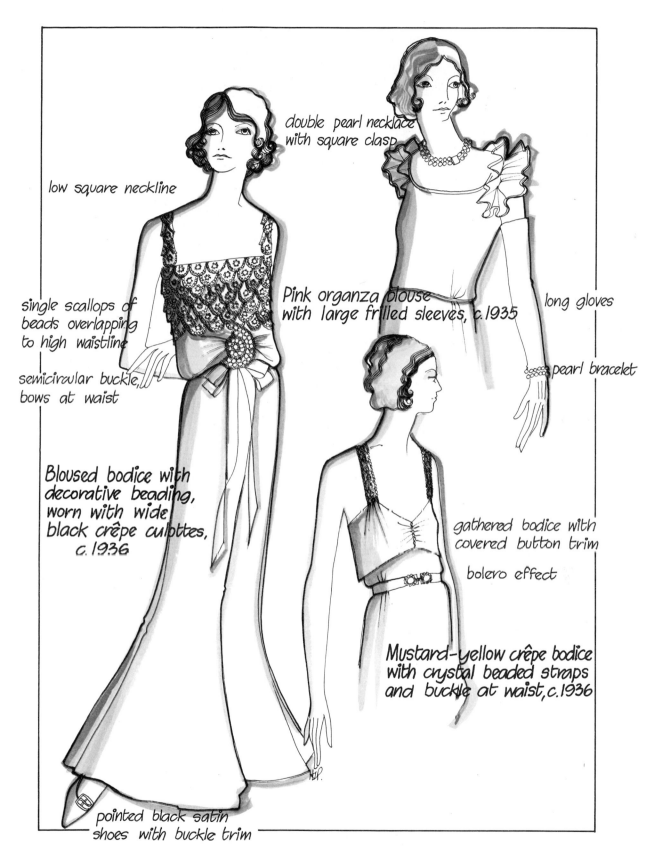

low square neckline

double pearl necklace
with square clasp

single scallops of
beads overlapping
to high waistline

Pink organza blouse
with large frilled sleeves, c.1935

long gloves

semicircular buckle,
bows at waist

pearl bracelet

Bloused bodice with
decorative beading,
worn with wide
black crêpe culottes,
c.1936

gathered bodice with
covered button trim

bolero effect

Mustard-yellow crêpe bodice
with crystal beaded straps
and buckle at waist, c.1936

pointed black satin
shoes with buckle trim

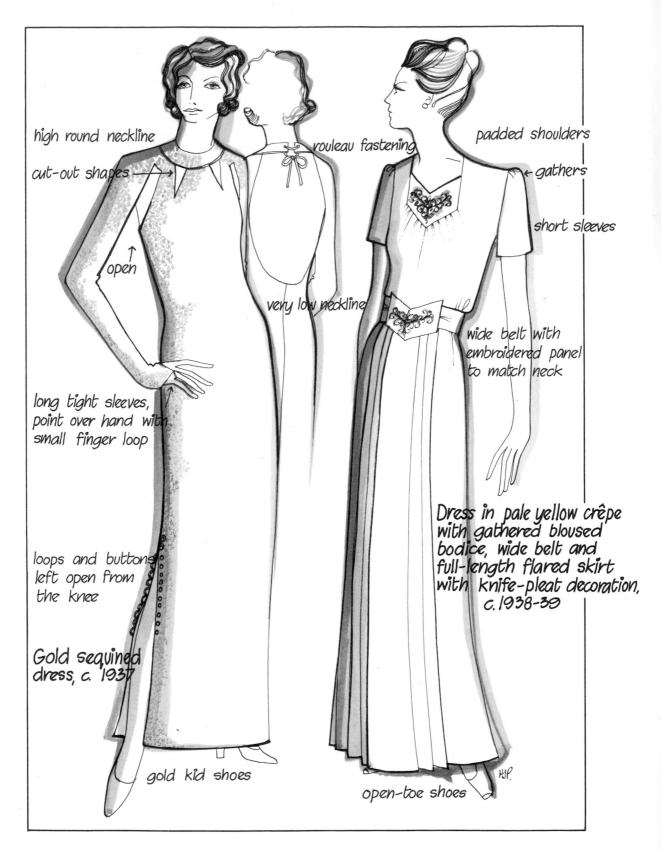

high round neckline

cut-out shapes

open

rouleau fastening

very low neckline

long tight sleeves, point over hand with small finger loop

loops and buttons left open from the knee

Gold sequined dress, c. 1937

gold kid shoes

padded shoulders

gathers

short sleeves

wide belt with embroidered panel to match neck

Dress in pale yellow crêpe with gathered bloused bodice, wide belt and full-length flared skirt with knife-pleat decoration, c. 1938-39

open-toe shoes

# WEDDING DRESSES c. 1930·32

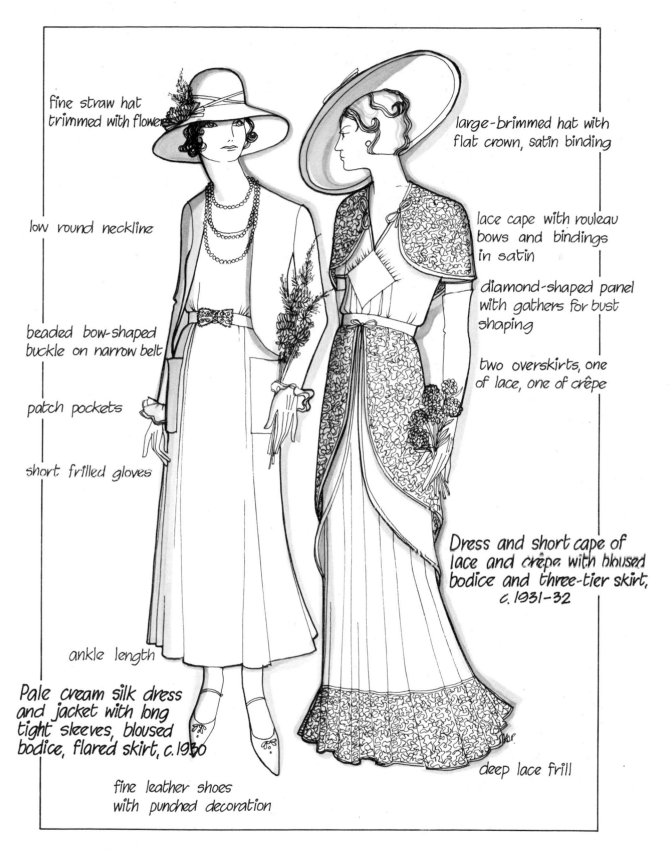

fine straw hat trimmed with flowers

low round neckline

beaded bow-shaped buckle on narrow belt

patch pockets

short frilled gloves

ankle length

Pale cream silk dress and jacket with long tight sleeves, bloused bodice, flared skirt, c. 1930

fine leather shoes with punched decoration

large-brimmed hat with flat crown, satin binding

lace cape with rouleau bows and bindings in satin

diamond-shaped panel with gathers for bust shaping

two overskirts, one of lace, one of crêpe

Dress and short cape of lace and crêpe with bloused bodice and three-tier skirt, c. 1931-32

deep lace frill

large hat decorated with silk roses

flat stylized bow

pintucked panel

dropped shoulder line, two bands of pintucks

embroidered flower design

puff sleeves

embroidered belt

lace edging

tiny covered buttons

headdress of tiny flowers and rouleau loops

fine chiffon veil

'V' shaped neckline with lace inserts

inset lace panels

draped cummerbund

long tight sleeves, tiny covered buttons to elbow

full train, lace trim

**White wedding dress with pale blue embroidery and pintucked panels, c. 1933**

**Silk dress with draped bodice and fine lace insertions, c. 1034**

# BRIDESMAIDS' DRESSES c.1935·36

turban-style hat with
large bow decoration

tie neckline

double cape-like
detail, seams and
tucks to waist

long tight sleeves

point over hand

inserted panels
to low hip

short train

large organza hat
with velvet trimming

wide circular-cut
collar and sleeves,
fine pleated edges

bow to one side
of neckline

wide belt, pleated edges

short gloves in fine
transparent fabric

skirt gathered over hips

ankle-length skirt

pleated hem

Stiff organza dress with
large collar and sleeves,
pleated decoration, c.1936

Fine pale blue crêpe dress with
cape-effect shoulder detail, bloused
bodice, wide bow tie belt, c.1935

# WEDDING DRESS c.1937·39

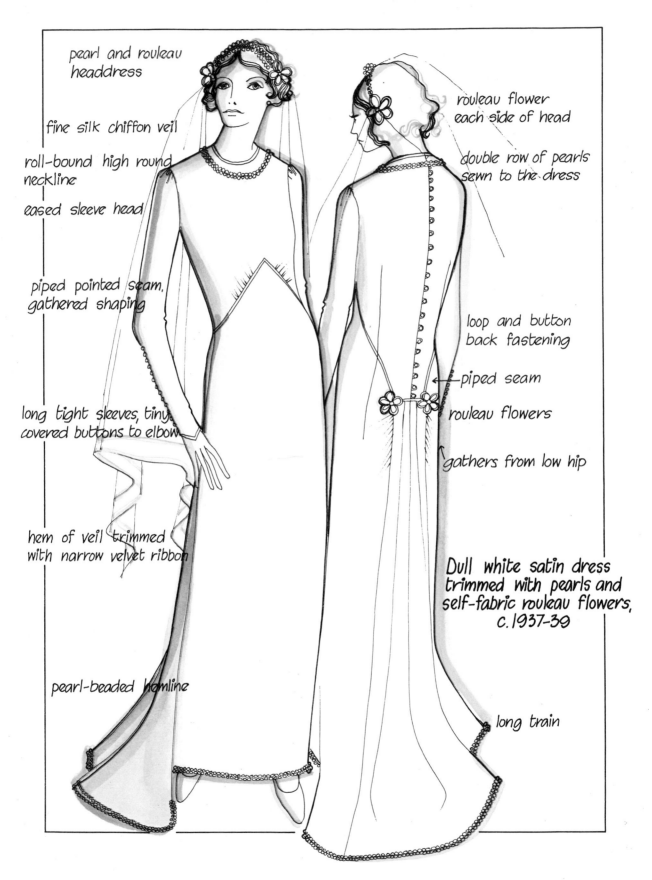

pearl and rouleau headdress

fine silk chiffon veil

roll-bound high round neckline

eased sleeve head

piped pointed seam, gathered shaping

long tight sleeves, tiny covered buttons to elbow

hem of veil trimmed with narrow velvet ribbon

pearl-beaded hemline

rouleau flower each side of head

double row of pearls sewn to the dress

loop and button back fastening

piped seam

rouleau flowers

gathers from low hip

Dull white satin dress trimmed with pearls and self-fabric rouleau flowers, c.1937-39

long train

soft fabric beret

beret with bow decoration

stiff tie-neck shirt

fox fur

asymmetric button-down collar

diagonal jacket fastening

twisted loop and button fastening

diamond-shaped panels at waist

gauntlet gloves

deep buttoned cuff

hip-length jacket

short gloves tucked under jacket cuff

seamed straight skirt with inverted box pleats

straight skirt with deep off-centre box pleat

mid-calf-length skirt

Grey flannel suit with long slim-fitting jacket, straight mid-calf-length skirt, c.1932

Beige wool bouclé suit with waist-length jacket, bold asymmetric detail, c.1930

glacé kid court shoes

elongated toes

# SUITS c.1933·34

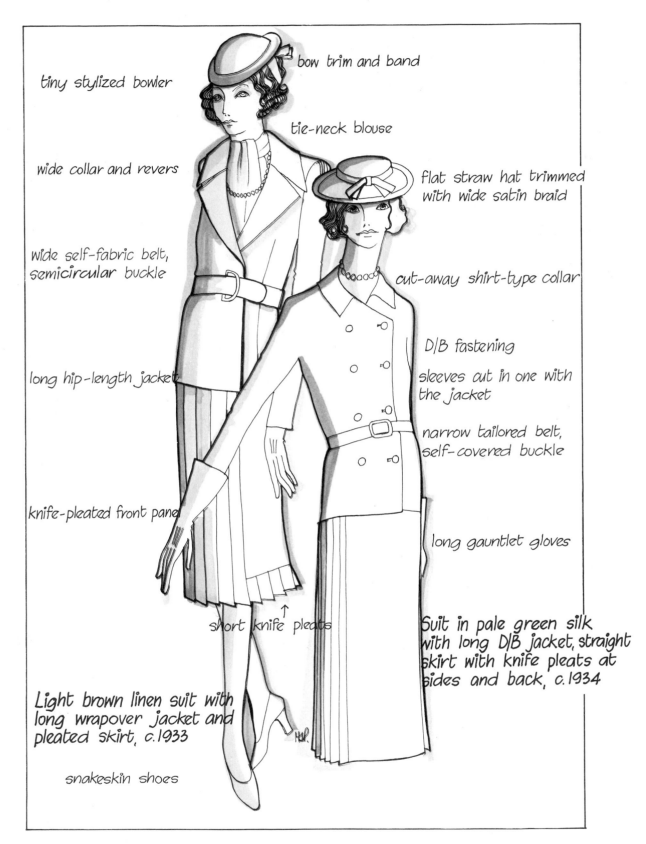

tiny stylized bowler

bow trim and band

tie-neck blouse

wide collar and revers

flat straw hat trimmed with wide satin braid

wide self-fabric belt, semicircular buckle

cut-away shirt-type collar

D/B fastening

long hip-length jacket

sleeves cut in one with the jacket

narrow tailored belt, self-covered buckle

knife-pleated front panel

long gauntlet gloves

short knife pleats

Suit in pale green silk with long D/B jacket, straight skirt with knife pleats at sides and back, c.1934

Light brown linen suit with long wrapover jacket and pleated skirt, c.1933

snakeskin shoes

# SUITS c. 1935·36

feather and bow trim

wide-brimmed felt hat

felt hat with bow trim worn on one side to front of head

notched collar, large brooch

top-stitching

gathered sleeve head

open jacket with fur trim over D/B waistcoat

soft belt

long tight sleeves with fur cuffs

turn-back cuff

short gloves

leather handbag

box-pleated skirt

box-pleated skirt

Suit with hip-length jacket, flared box-pleated skirt, c. 1935

Rust-coloured wool suit with waistcoat and short jacket trimmed with fox fur, c. 1936

two-tone shoes

shoes with buttoned canvas insert

# SUITS c. 1937·39

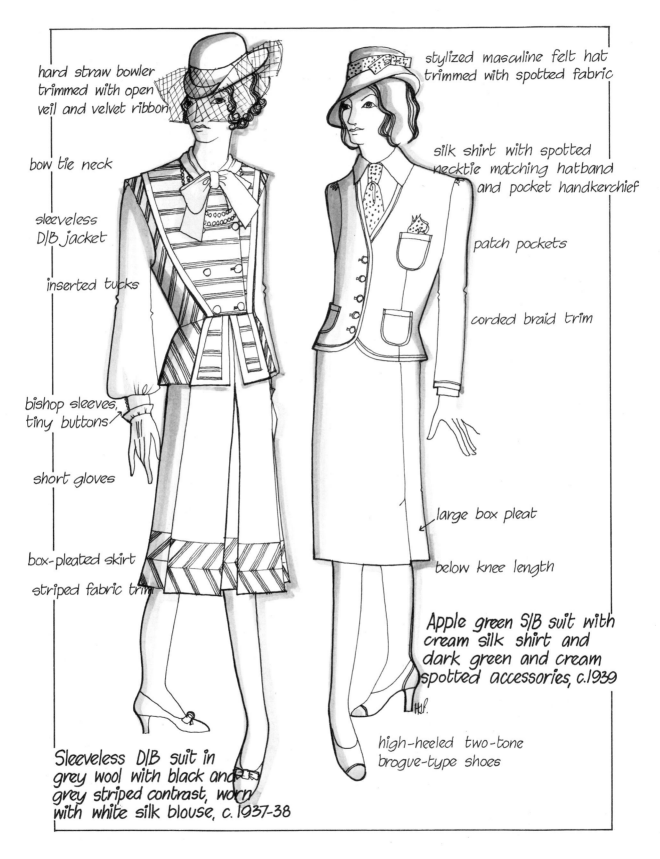

hard straw bowler
trimmed with open
veil and velvet ribbon

bow tie neck

sleeveless
D/B jacket

inserted tucks

bishop sleeves,
tiny buttons

short gloves

box-pleated skirt

striped fabric trim

stylized masculine felt hat
trimmed with spotted fabric

silk shirt with spotted
necktie matching hatband
and pocket handkerchief

patch pockets

corded braid trim

large box pleat

below knee length

**Apple green S/B suit with
cream silk shirt and
dark green and cream
spotted accessories, c.1939**

high-heeled two-tone
brogue-type shoes

**Sleeveless D/B suit in
grey wool with black and
grey striped contrast, worn
with white silk blouse, c.1937-38**

velvet hat with side bow trimming

small round beret

gathered sleeve head

large fur collar

scalloped revers

short scalloped oversleeve

belt with single button fastening

D/B fastening

deep scalloped cuff

waterfall wrapover trimmed with fur

Pink fine wool coat with scalloped decoration, slim bodice, flared skirt, c.1932

two-tone shoes, thick heels

Bright red wool coat trimmed with smooth black fur, c.1930

# COATS c.1933·34

hard felt hat with braid trim

small hat worn on one side of the head

striped scarf

darts →

long peter pan collar

leg-of-mutton sleeves

large flat collar

loops and buttons

belt from side seam

wide belt

long buttoned cuff

welt pockets

sleeves eased into a cuff

D/B fastening to above knee length

flared skirt

ankle-length skirt

suede shoes, bow decoration

Slim-fitting D/B coat with low button detail, slim skirt flaring from knee level, c.1934

Edge-to-edge coat with large collar, loop and button fastening at belt and neck, c.1933

flat saucer-shaped hat worn
on the front of the head

double tie collar in fur

fur epaulettes

padded shoulders

four buttoned
welt pockets

wrapover front

wide belt, round buckle

narrow fur trim

deep turn-back cuffs

panel seams from
shoulder to hem

coat worn with trousers

brown court shoes
← banded with cream

Wrapover coat with appliqué felt
flowers in a border down the front
edge and on the cuffs, c. 1936

S/B cream wool coat with
brown fur trimming at neck
and wrist, c. 1935-36

flat low crown

wide-brimmed hat
with bow trim

asymmetric-
brimmed straw hat,
ribbon trim

tie neck

wide roll collar

high yoke seam

tailored belt

flower-shaped
plastic buttons

welt pockets with
bow decoration

bound cuffs

patch pockets

3/4 length

7/8 length →

Heavy cotton gaberdine coat
worn over lightweight spotted
cotton dress, c. 1939

Three-quarter-length coat with
wide binding on roll collar,
cuffs and pockets, c. 1937-38

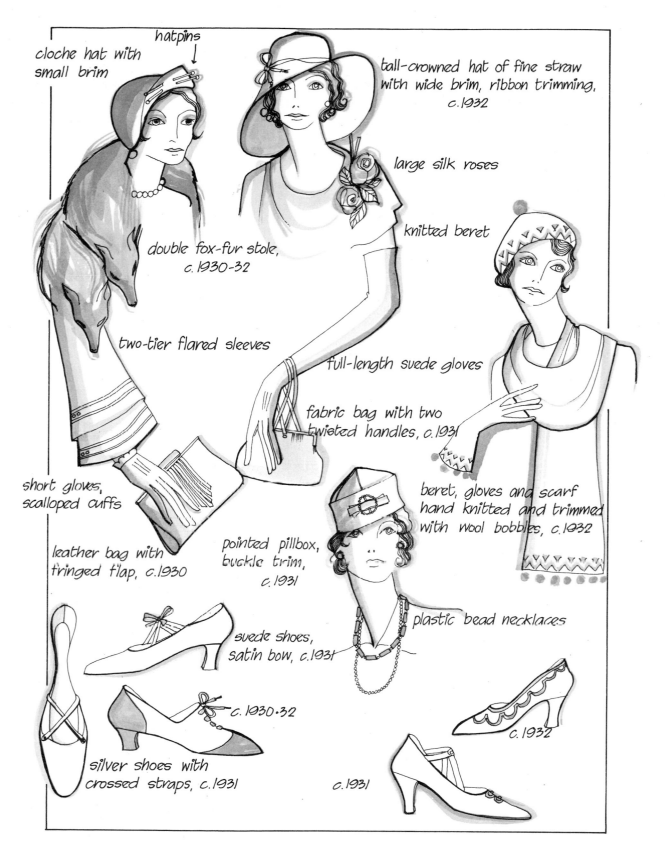

cloche hat with small brim

hatpins

tall-crowned hat of fine straw with wide brim, ribbon trimming, c.1932

large silk roses

knitted beret

double fox-fur stole, c.1930-32

two-tier flared sleeves

full-length suede gloves

fabric bag with two twisted handles, c.1931

short gloves, scalloped cuffs

beret, gloves and scarf hand knitted and trimmed with wool bobbles, c.1932

leather bag with fringed flap, c.1930

pointed pillbox, buckle trim, c.1931

plastic bead necklaces

suede shoes, satin bow, c.1931

c.1930·32

c.1932

silver shoes with crossed straps, c.1931

c.1931

domed felt hat,
threaded felt
bow decoration,
c.1933

large plastic
beads

straw boater with wide
ribbon and large bow decoration,
c.1933

front-tilted straw
hat, looped ribbon
trim at the back

gloves, c.1933

plastic bangles

fur-trimmed gloves

scarf clip

scarf with bound
edges and delicate
embroidery

large picture hat with
organza flowers, c.1934

pillbox hat with rouleau
loop tassel, c.1934

back-tied neckscarf

soft suede
handbag

matching beret
and scarf in red
and white spotted
silk, c.1934

long stiff detachable
cotton cuffs, c.1933

62

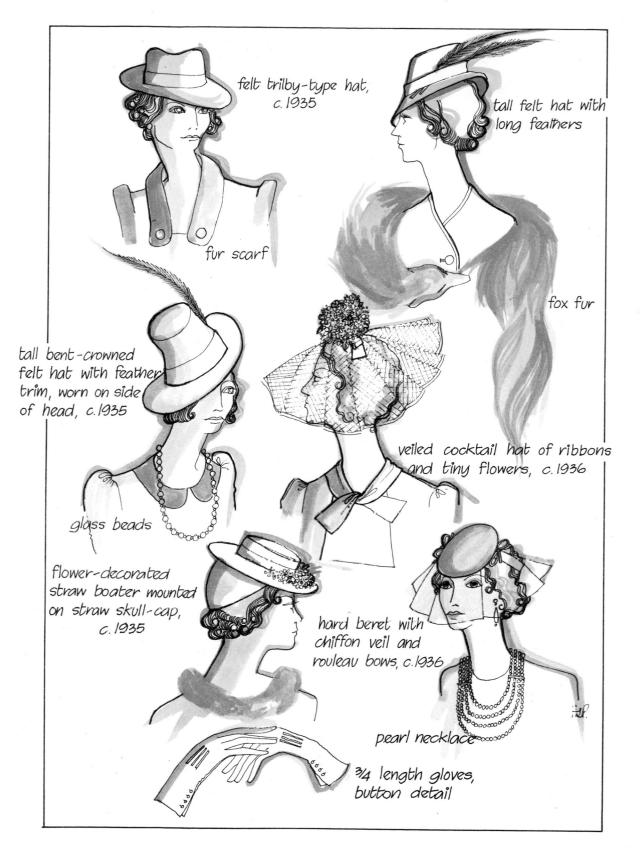

felt trilby-type hat, c. 1935

tall felt hat with long feathers

fur scarf

fox fur

tall bent-crowned felt hat with feather trim, worn on side of head, c. 1935

glass beads

veiled cocktail hat of ribbons and tiny flowers, c. 1936

flower-decorated straw boater mounted on straw skull-cap, c. 1935

hard beret with chiffon veil and rouleau bows, c. 1936

pearl necklace

¾ length gloves, button detail

small monkey-skin hat, c. 1937-38

padded shoulders

stylized beret with wide fabric streamers and corded tassels, c. 1939

fur buttons on underdress

straw hat with velvet and flower trim, c. 1938

monkey-fur coat, c. 1938

long embroidered mittens, c. 1937

flowers

fine veil

evening hat, c. 1939

fox-fur cape with velvet ties, c. 1939

felt hat with punched hole decoration, c. 1939

collar and gloves to match hat

c. 1937·39

c. 1937·38

c. 1939

c. 1938·39

c. 1939

HSL.

64

glass beads

sweetheart neckline

gathers, rouleau bow decoration

wide collar

shoulder pads

covered buttons

patch pockets

plaited wool decoration

short sleeves

bloused bodice

tailored belt and covered buckle

wide belt, covered buckle

large patch pockets

knee-length gathered skirt

flared skirt, double box pleats

Crêpe dress with low neckline decorated with rouleau bows, bloused bodice, full gathered skirt, c. 1940

Lilac wool dress with button-through bodice, knee-length flared skirt, c. 1941

suede shoes, high heels

court shoes, flat bow decoration

peter pan collar, flat bow tie trim

high yoke seam, gathers over bustline

gathered sleeve head

covered buttons

tailored belt

short set-in sleeves, wide turn-back cuffs

bow trim

welt pockets

long tight sleeves, button trim at wrist

channel seams

flared skirt

Heavy cotton day dress with panel seams from shoulder to hem forming knife pleats above knee, c. 1943

Collarless linen dress with high yoke seam, covered buttons, fabric belt, C/F seam and inverted box pleat, c.1944

Crisp linen dress with seamed button-through bodice, set-in waistband, skirt with 'V' shaped seams, C/F box pleat, c.1943

# DAY DRESSES c. 1945·46

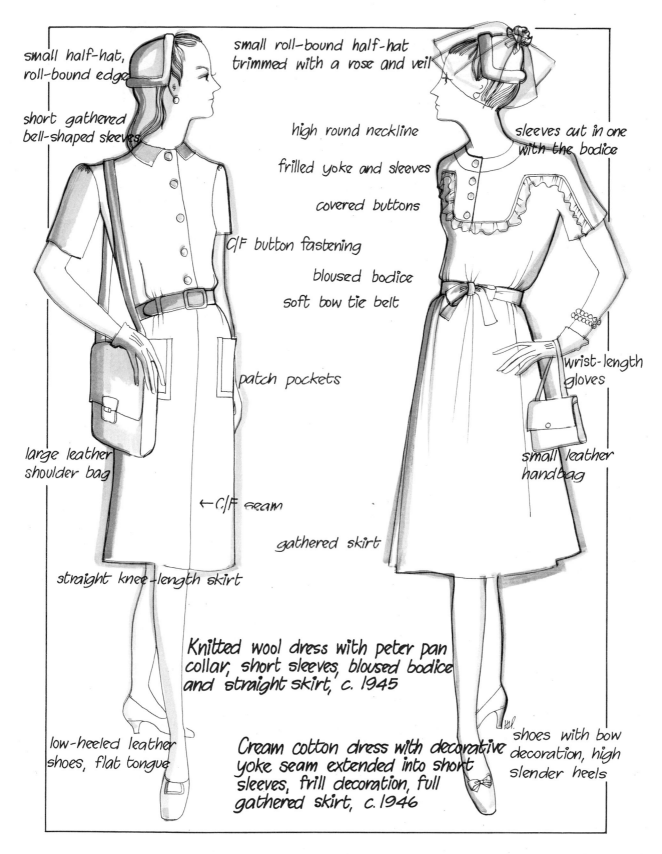

small half-hat, roll-bound edge

small roll-bound half-hat trimmed with a rose and veil

short gathered bell-shaped sleeves

high round neckline

frilled yoke and sleeves

covered buttons

C/F button fastening

bloused bodice

soft bow tie belt

sleeves cut in one with the bodice

wrist-length gloves

patch pockets

large leather shoulder bag

small leather handbag

← C/F seam

gathered skirt

straight knee-length skirt

Knitted wool dress with peter pan collar, short sleeves, bloused bodice and straight skirt, c. 1945

low-heeled leather shoes, flat tongue

Cream cotton dress with decorative yoke seam extended into short sleeves, frill decoration, full gathered skirt, c.1946

shoes with bow decoration, high slender heels

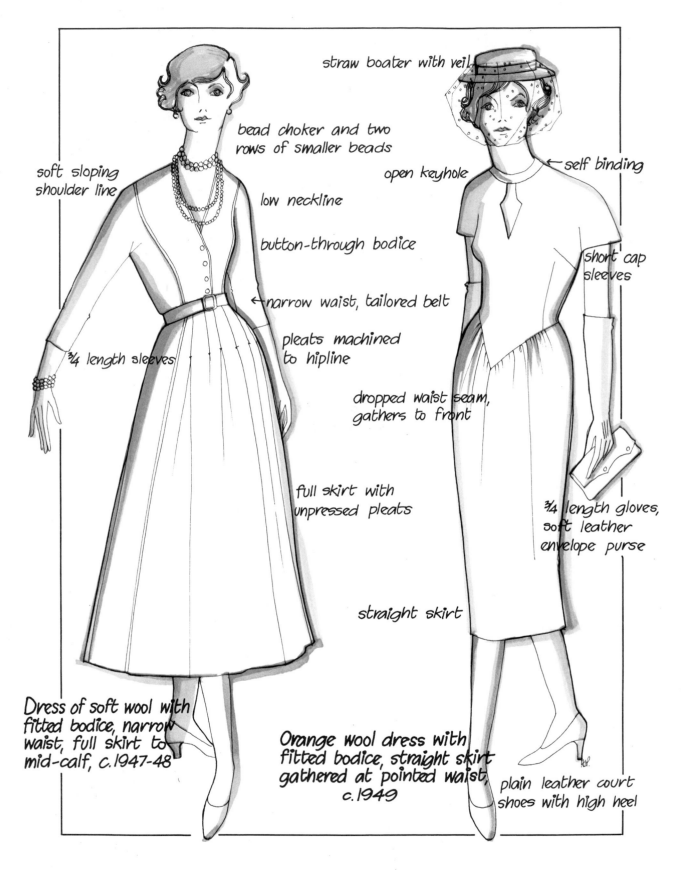

straw boater with veil

bead choker and two
rows of smaller beads

soft sloping
shoulder line

low neckline

open keyhole

self binding

button-through bodice

narrow waist, tailored belt

short cap
sleeves

pleats machined
to hipline

¾ length sleeves

dropped waist seam,
gathers to front

full skirt with
unpressed pleats

¾ length gloves,
soft leather
envelope purse

straight skirt

Dress of soft wool with
fitted bodice, narrow
waist, full skirt to
mid-calf, c. 1947-48

Orange wool dress with
fitted bodice, straight skirt
gathered at pointed waist,
c. 1949

plain leather court
shoes with high heel

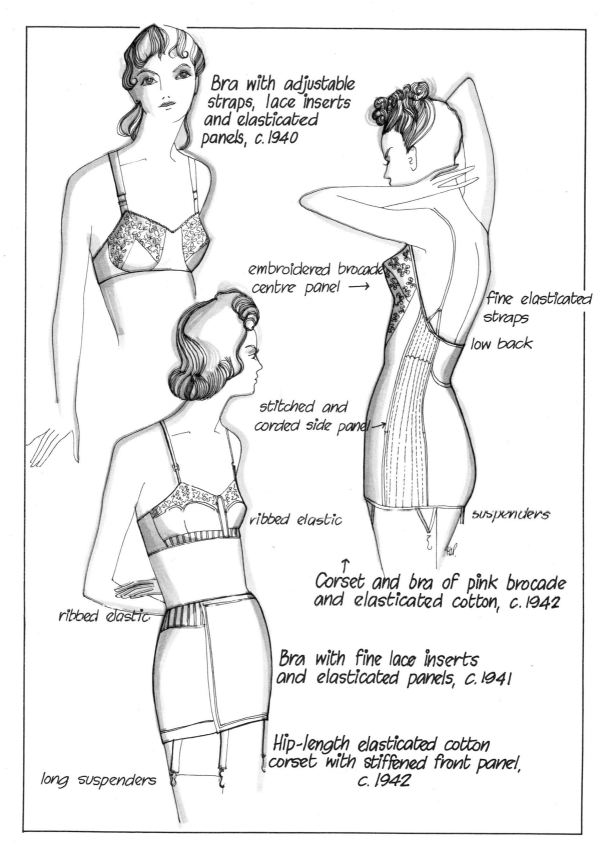

Bra with adjustable
straps, lace inserts
and elasticated
panels, c.1940

embroidered brocade
centre panel →

fine elasticated
straps

low back

stitched and
corded side panel →

ribbed elastic

suspenders

ribbed elastic

Corset and bra of pink brocade
and elasticated cotton, c.1942

Bra with fine lace inserts
and elasticated panels, c.1941

Hip-length elasticated cotton
corset with stiffened front panel,
c.1942

long suspenders

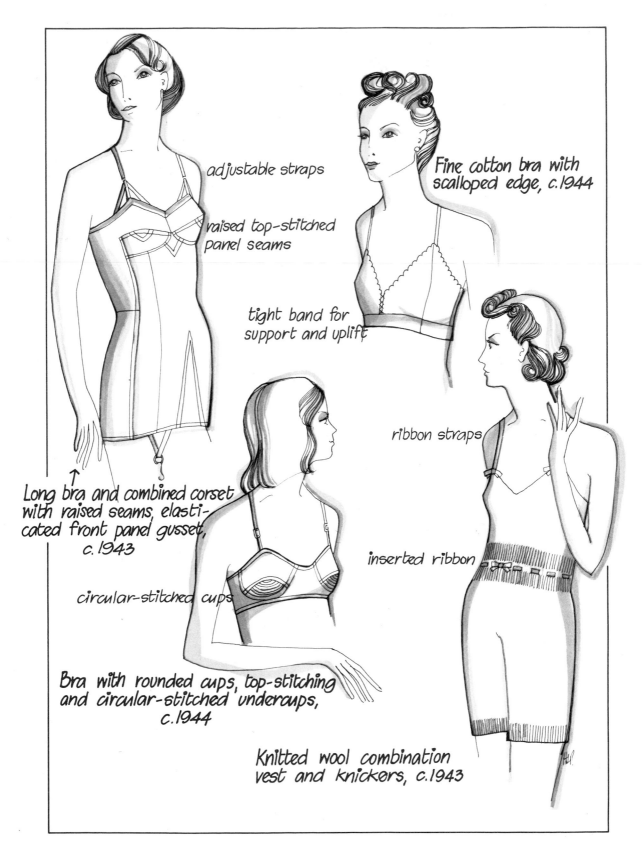

adjustable straps

raised top-stitched panel seams

Fine cotton bra with scalloped edge, c.1944

tight band for support and uplift

Long bra and combined corset with raised seams, elasti- cated front panel gusset, c.1943

ribbon straps

inserted ribbon

circular-stitched cups

Bra with rounded cups, top-stitching and circular-stitched undercups, c.1944

Knitted wool combination vest and knickers, c.1943

wide shoulder straps

wide satin ribbon
shoulder straps

pintucks

wide stitched shoulder straps

stitched decoration

bra and knickers with
D/B button fastening

diamond-shaped
stitched decoration

wide flared knickers

Princess-line petticoat
with lace inserts and
lace trimming at bust
and hem, c.1945

Short white satin nightdress
with high waist, gathered bust
shaping and wide satin belt
from side darts to C/B, c.1946

Matching bra and knickers with
stitched decoration and button
detail, c.1946

satin slippers with
rouleau bow decoration

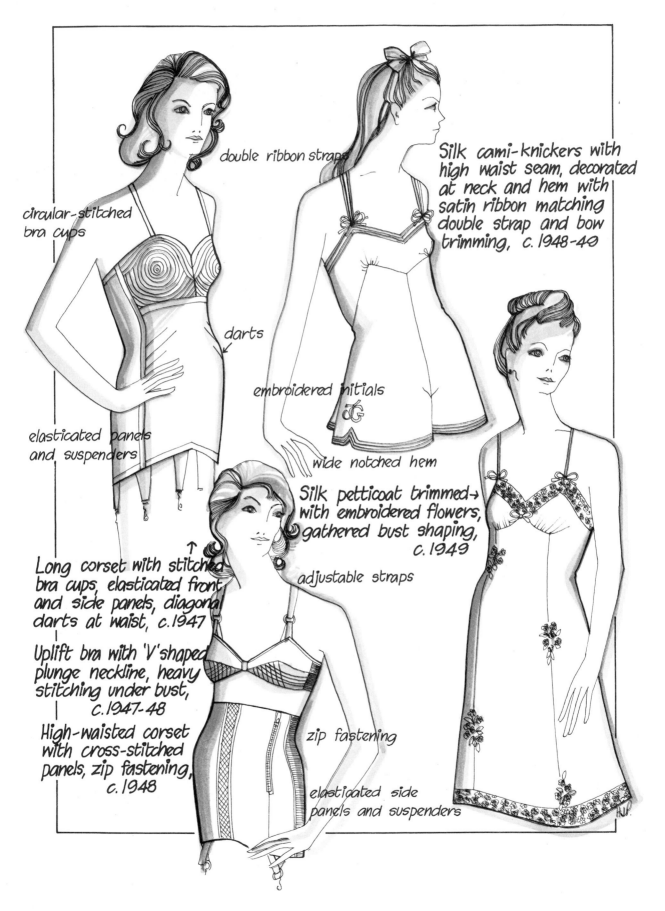

double ribbon straps

circular-stitched bra cups

darts

elasticated panels and suspenders

Silk cami-knickers with high waist seam, decorated at neck and hem with satin ribbon matching double strap and bow trimming, c.1948-49

embroidered initials

wide notched hem

Silk petticoat trimmed→ with embroidered flowers, gathered bust shaping, c.1949

adjustable straps

Long corset with stitched bra cups, elasticated front and side panels, diagonal darts at waist, c.1947

Uplift bra with 'V'shaped plunge neckline, heavy stitching under bust, c.1947-48

High-waisted corset with cross-stitched panels, zip fastening, c.1948

zip fastening

elasticated side panels and suspenders

padded shoulders

inset bands matching hem and pockets

C/F zip

wide belt, covered buckle

long set-in sleeves, inset band

**Collarless hand-knitted cardigan with C/F zip fastener, waist-level flap pockets, c. 1940**

wide shoulder strap

high yoke

gathers over bust

hip basque

full skirt

**Cotton sundress with top-stitched shoulder straps, yoke, belt and hip basque, c. 1942**

padded and darted shoulder

set-in sleeve

long peter pan collar

C/F zip fastener

decorative button trim

turn-back cuff

**Slim-fitting knitted cardigan with C/F zip-fastener, patch pockets set into a side panel, c.1941-42**

small wool hat with wired edge and tassel trimming

gathered shirt sleeve

shirt collar
covered buttons

gathered sleeve

square neckline

pinafore top

patch pocket

fitted waistcoat

flap pockets

sleeve gathered into narrow cuff

bishop-type sleeves, long narrow cuff

wrapover skirt

Waistcoat and trouser suit of soft camel-coloured wool worn with a cream and blue spotted silk shirt, c.1943-44

knee length

straight-cut trousers with C/F crease

knee-length canvas spats worn over flat leather shoes

narrow turnups

soft leather brogue-type shoes with platform soles

Grey tweed pinafore dress with wrapover skirt, patch pockets, decorative top-stitching, c.1944

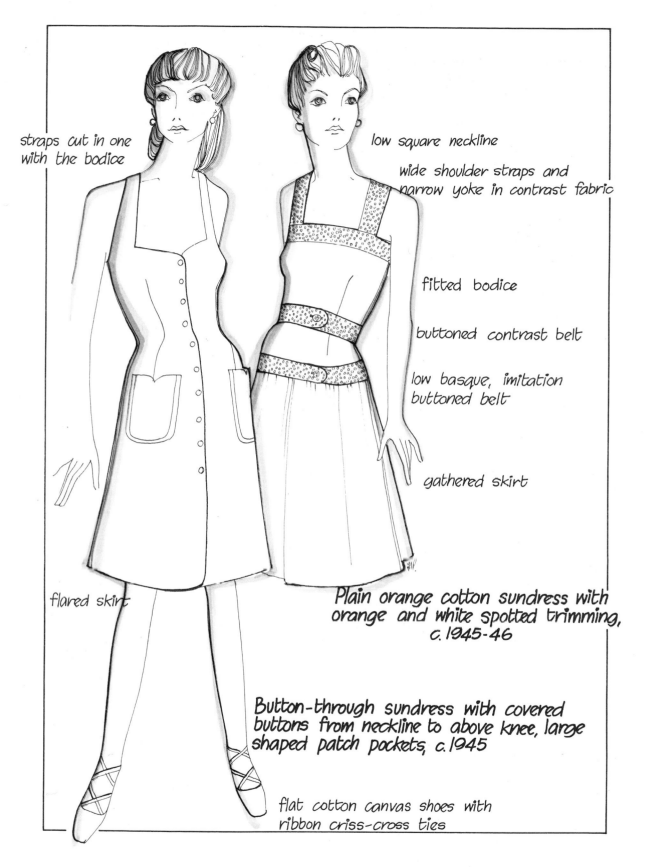

straps cut in one
with the bodice

low square neckline

wide shoulder straps and
narrow yoke in contrast fabric

fitted bodice

buttoned contrast belt

low basque, imitation
buttoned belt

gathered skirt

flared skirt

Plain orange cotton sundress with
orange and white spotted trimming,
c.1945-46

Button-through sundress with covered
buttons from neckline to above knee, large
shaped patch pockets, c.1945

flat cotton canvas shoes with
ribbon criss-cross ties

narrow rouleau straps

tiny shirt buttons

collar with small self-fabric ties

gathers and dart shaping

extended shoulder seam

sleeveless jacket

narrow waistband

buttoned patch pockets

full bishop sleeves gathered into a cuff

Black and red wool check jacket worn with black wool trousers and matching shirt, c.1948·49

trousers with C/F crease

Cotton bikini top and shorts with contrast rouleau bindings, c.1947-48

cotton canvas sandals with ribbon straps

brogue-type shoes

turnups

# EVENING DRESSES c.1940·42

silk flowers

low square neckline, wide straps

pleated binding

bias-cut striped bodice

long french dart

silk flowers

striped binding

chiffon overskirts

silver evening shoes, button and bow trim

**Navy blue and silver evening dress with tight-fitting bodice, transparent tiered overskirt and plain blue silk underskirt, c.1940·41**

plaited shoulder straps

silk flowers

ruched bodice

pleated chiffon belt

long gloves

plain silk underskirt

**Black silk underdress covered with black silk chiffon, c.1942**

hem bound in pleated chiffon

silver strap sandals

wide shoulder line
with padding

deep 'V' shaped neckline

large lace puff sleeves

C/F seam with
ruched shaping

high waist seam

large stiff lace bow

low neckline

rouleau band
and bow tie

Cotton evening dress with
high-seamed bodice, lace
trimming, c.1944

floor-length skirt

Yellow-orange crêpe dress with
large bishop sleeves, ruched
bodice, wide belt and diamanté
buckle, soft gathered skirt,
c.1943

full gathered skirt with lace bands

# EVENING DRESSES c.1945·46

silk organza flowers

evening hat decorated with hearts and flowers

lace sleeves and yoke

bound neck edge

inserted frill

flesh-coloured shoulder pads

low 'V' shaped neckline

embroidered bodice

embroidered hearts and flowers following shape of neckline

narrow tailored belt

belt

'V' shaped waist seam

tiny buttons

long embroidered mittens →

pleats sewn to low hip level

knife-pleated floor-length skirt

narrow box pleats

strap sandals

Black crêpe dress with long tight lace sleeves and fine black silk embroidered bodice, c.1945

Turquoise crêpe dress, gloves and hat embroidered with copper-coloured silk flowers and heart-shaped sequins, c.1946

79

large artificial flowers

low square neckline

draped cape sleeves
with shoulder pads

beaded clips

curved waist seam

gathers over hips

C/F seam and knife pleat

long bead earrings
matching necklace

low neckline

turn-down collar

C/F button fastening

curved waist seam

full gathered skirt

full-length tight
sleeves curved
over hand

Crêpe dress with draped
sleeves and neckline,
fitted bodice, long slim
skirt, c. 1947-48

ankle length

Dark red velvet evening dress
with low neckline, mock collar,
tight-fitting bodice and full skirt,
c. 1949

white felt hat with organza roses

flower and ribbon headdress, short fine silk veil

padded shoulders

padded shoulders

gathers

sweetheart neckline

C/F ruched panel

decorative seaming

¾ length sleeves

organza roses

tiny covered buttons to elbow

dropped waistline

slim bias-cut skirt

point over hand

knee length

Heavy silk dress with sweetheart neckline, slim-fitting ruched bodice, gathered skirt, c.1940

white suede shoes, peep toes

Dress in dull satin with decorative seaming, bias-cut skirt, c.1942

cross-strap sandals

# WEDDING DRESSES c. 1943·44

tiny flowers arranged in the hair, waist-length veil

single flower headdress shoulder-length veil

padded and gathered shoulders

gathered panel

rounded half-yoke

short jacket

gathers above and below bust

wide gathered sleeve head

corded detail

gathered bra-like detail on dress

bow-tied sash

fitted bodice

cord

long tight sleeves point over hand

flared sleeve

gathered panel

long rounded train

knee-length skirt

pale-coloured nylon stockings

cream suede shoes with roll buckle and high slim heels

White dull satin wedding dress with high waist seam, tight-fitting bodice, slim skirt with a long train, c.1943

Suit of cream crêpe with short jacket, dress with gathered panel over the bust, flared skirt, gathered side panels, c.1944

# WEDDING DRESS c.1945·46

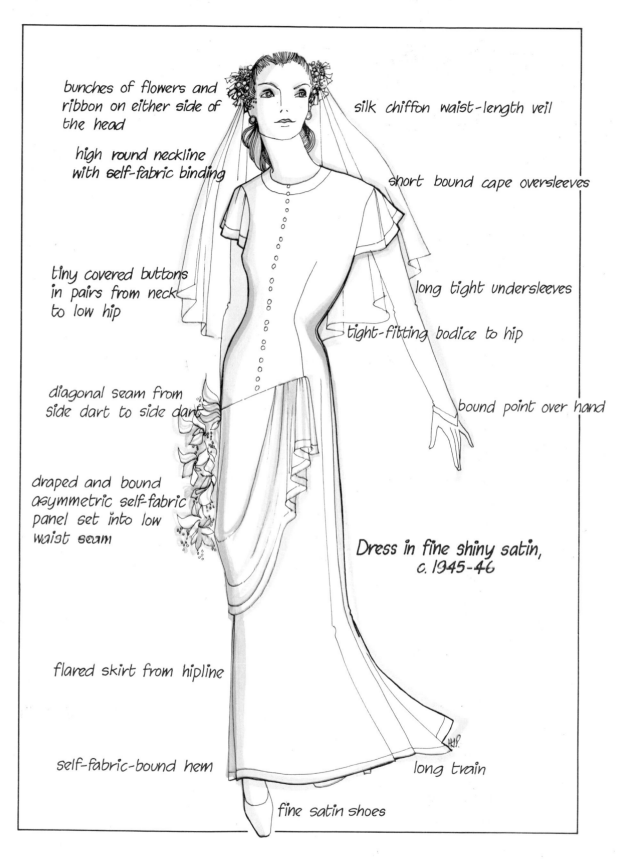

bunches of flowers and ribbon on either side of the head

silk chiffon waist-length veil

high round neckline with self-fabric binding

short bound cape oversleeves

tiny covered buttons in pairs from neck to low hip

long tight undersleeves

tight-fitting bodice to hip

diagonal seam from side dart to side dart

bound point over hand

draped and bound asymmetric self-fabric panel set into low waist seam

Dress in fine shiny satin, c. 1945-46

flared skirt from hipline

self-fabric-bound hem

long train

fine satin shoes

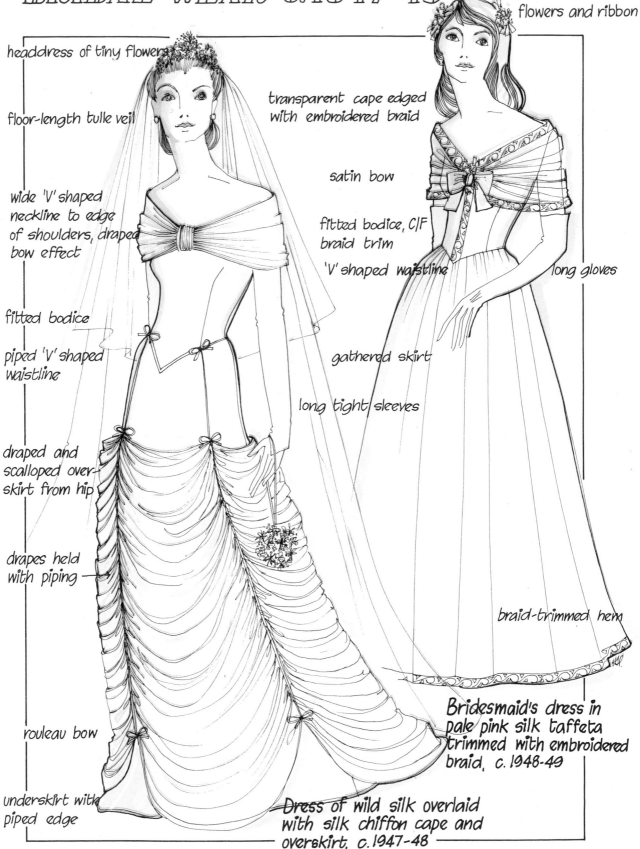

flowers and ribbon

headdress of tiny flowers

floor-length tulle veil

transparent cape edged with embroidered braid

satin bow

wide 'V' shaped neckline to edge of shoulders, draped bow effect

fitted bodice, C/F braid trim

'V' shaped waistline

long gloves

fitted bodice

piped 'V' shaped waistline

gathered skirt

long tight sleeves

draped and scalloped over-skirt from hip

drapes held with piping

braid-trimmed hem

Bridesmaid's dress in pale pink silk taffeta trimmed with embroidered braid. c.1948-49

rouleau bow

underskirt with piped edge

Dress of wild silk overlaid with silk chiffon cape and overskirt, c.1947-48

hard felt hat, braid trim

shirt collar

strap opening

collar and revers in contrast colour

domed hat, flower trim

puff sleeves

peter pan collar

braid bow tie

contrast cuff and belt

diagonal welt pockets

bloused jacket

flared skirt, C/F inverted box pleat

gauntlet gloves

flared skirt

flared skirt, braided seam

**Wool suit in diagonal check with contrast collar, cuffs and tailored belt, c. 1940-41**

**Plain wool dress and striped jacket, all seams and panels trimmed with narrow braid, c. 1940**

**Dress and short jacket in soft wool with contrast details, c. 1942**

high-heeled brogue-type shoes

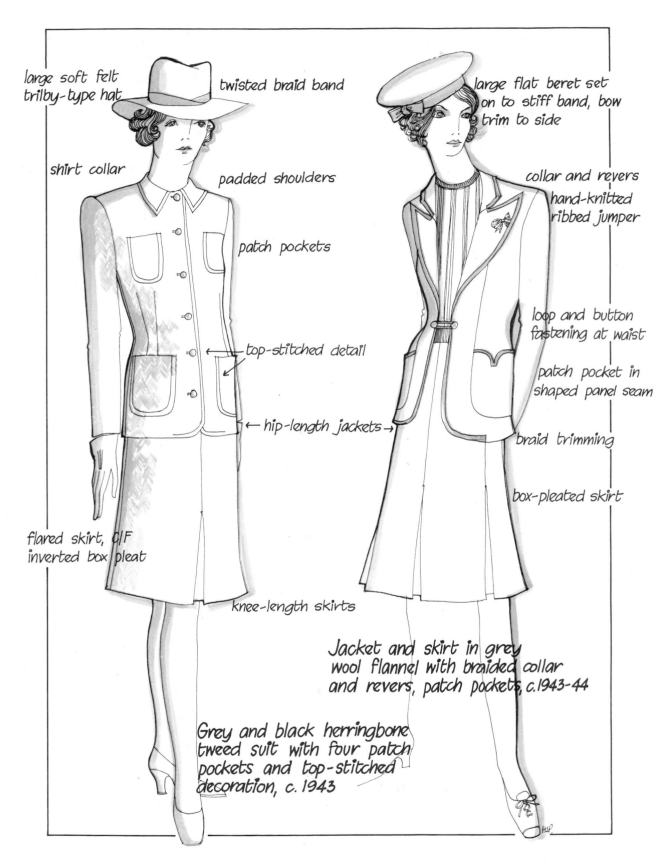

large soft felt
trilby-type hat

twisted braid band

large flat beret set
on to stiff band, bow
trim to side

shirt collar

padded shoulders

collar and revers

hand-knitted
ribbed jumper

patch pockets

top-stitched detail

loop and button
fastening at waist

patch pocket in
shaped panel seam

← hip-length jackets →

braid trimming

box-pleated skirt

flared skirt, C/F
inverted box pleat

knee-length skirts

Jacket and skirt in grey
wool flannel with braided collar
and revers, patch pockets, c.1943-44

Grey and black herringbone
tweed suit with four patch
pockets and top-stitched
decoration, c.1943

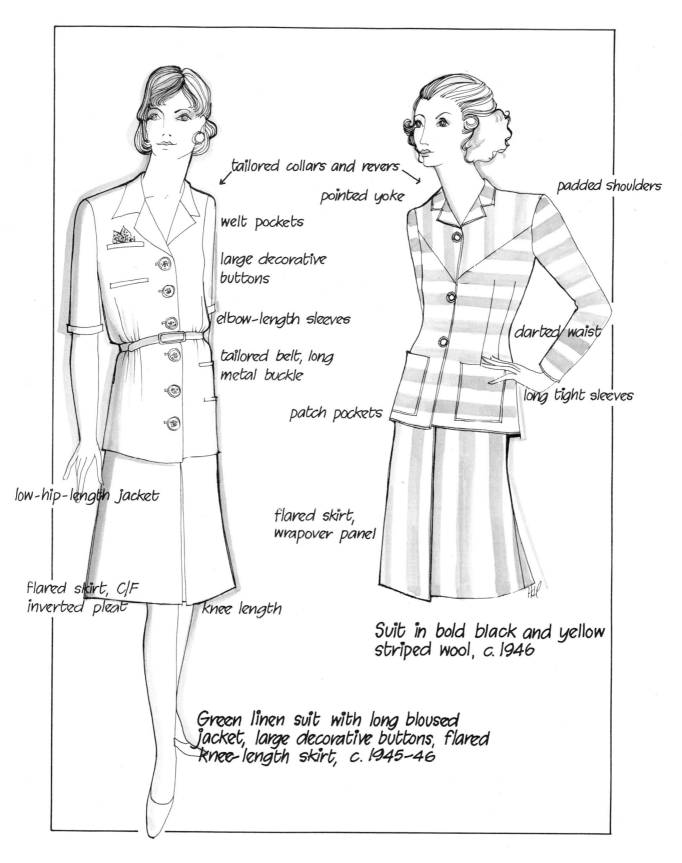

tailored collars and revers

pointed yoke

welt pockets

large decorative buttons

elbow-length sleeves

tailored belt, long metal buckle

patch pockets

low-hip-length jacket

flared skirt, C/F inverted pleat

knee length

padded shoulders

darted waist

long tight sleeves

flared skirt, wrapover panel

Suit in bold black and yellow striped wool, c.1946

Green linen suit with long bloused jacket, large decorative buttons, flared knee-length skirt, c.1945–46

hard felt skull-cap
silk poppy trim

narrow headband with
tiny bow trimming

shallow grown-on
collar

peter pan collar with
bow tie trimming

soft unpadded
shoulder line

side button fastening
from shoulder to
low waist

tight-fitting bodice

short sleeves

narrow waist

small waist, narrow
tailored belt

two-tier notched
jacket skirt

hip-length jacket

large leather handbag

small leather handbag

mid-calf-length flared skirt

flared skirt

Rough wool suit with
long fitted jacket, short
sleeves, c.1948-49

Fine wool suit,
c.1947-48

suede shoes with
two ankle straps

ankle-strap shoes

# COATS c. 1940·42

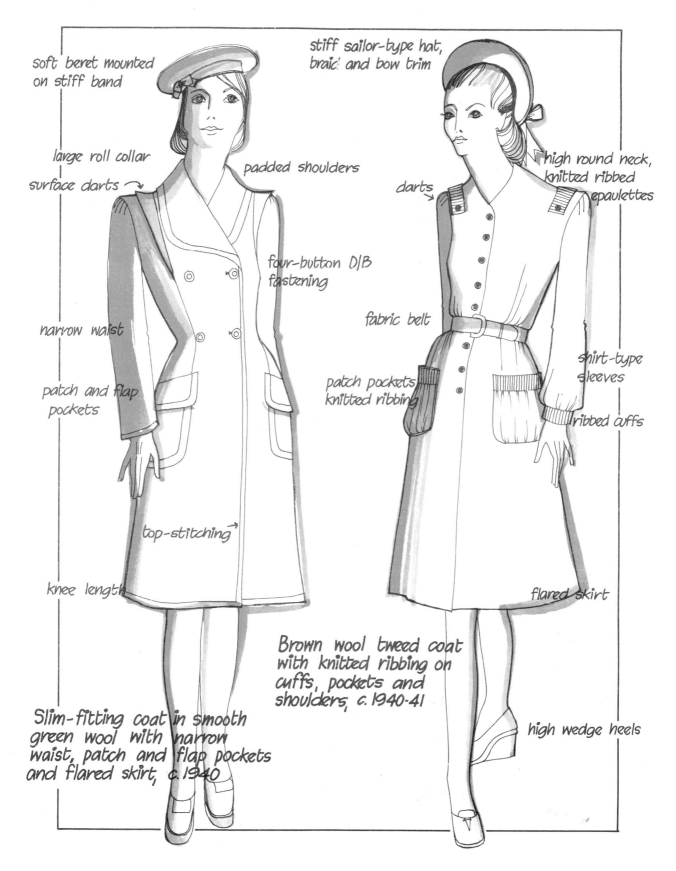

soft beret mounted on stiff band

stiff sailor-type hat, braid and bow trim

large roll collar

surface darts

padded shoulders

darts

high round neck, knitted ribbed epaulettes

four-button D/B fastening

narrow waist

fabric belt

shirt-type sleeves

patch and flap pockets

patch pockets knitted ribbing

ribbed cuffs

top-stitching

knee length

flared skirt

Brown wool tweed coat with knitted ribbing on cuffs, pockets and shoulders, c. 1940-41

Slim-fitting coat in smooth green wool with narrow waist, patch and flap pockets and flared skirt, c. 1940

high wedge heels

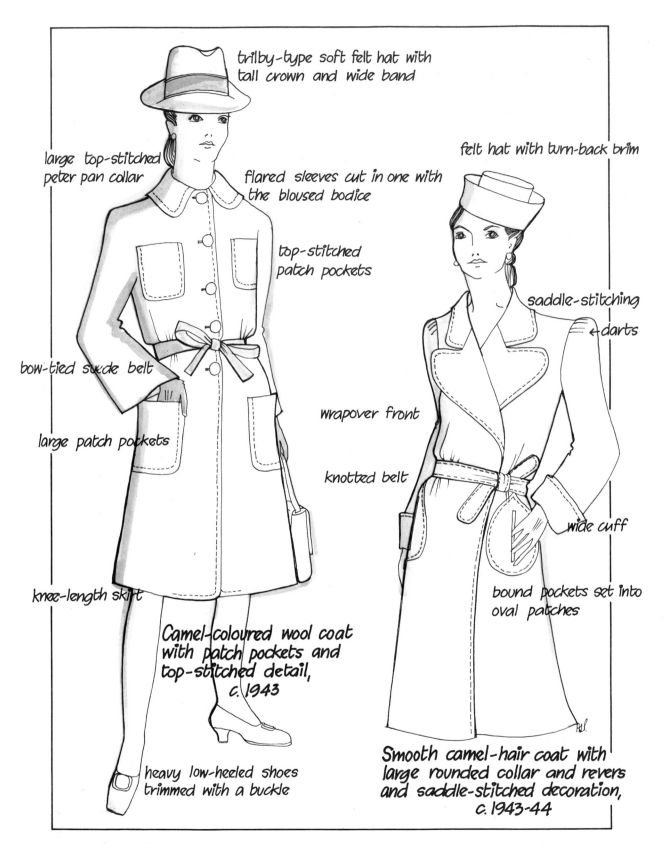

trilby-type soft felt hat with tall crown and wide band

felt hat with turn-back brim

large top-stitched peter pan collar

flared sleeves cut in one with the bloused bodice

top-stitched patch pockets

saddle-stitching

darts

bow-tied suede belt

wrapover front

knotted belt

large patch pockets

wide cuff

knee-length skirt

bound pockets set into oval patches

Camel-coloured wool coat with patch pockets and top-stitched detail, c.1943

heavy low-heeled shoes trimmed with a buckle

Smooth camel-hair coat with large rounded collar and revers and saddle-stitched decoration, c.1943-44

# COATS c.1945·46

stiff felt hat, wide looped ribbon trim

wool beret with butterfly brooch

wide padded and darted shoulder

channel seam

rounded stand collar

inverted box pleat

pads and darts

high yoke

braid trim

leather belt

channel-slot seams

wide cuff

pads

wide bishop-type sleeves, deep cuff

half-yoke

inverted box pleats

Short flared wool coat with deep C/B inverted box pleat, wide sleeves and turn-back cuffs, c.1945-46

Smooth slim-fitting coat with shaped panel seams and fine braid trimming, c.1946

Heavy dark blue linen coat with channel seams from yoke to hip, c.1945-46

soft felt hat with long feathers

hood with turn-back cuff

high pointed stand collar

edge-to-edge front

wide revers

sleeves cut in one with the bodice

hook and eye fastening

surface darts

wide sleeves cut in one with the bodice

threaded leather belt

D/B fastening

flared sleeve

buttoned belt

sleeve gathered into a wide cuff

large patch pockets

flared box pleats

ankle-length skirt

mid-calf-length skirt

**Orange wool coat with narrow waist and full skirt, c.1947-48**

rain boots with C/F zip fastening, high heels

**D/B gaberdine raincoat with attached hood, c.1949**

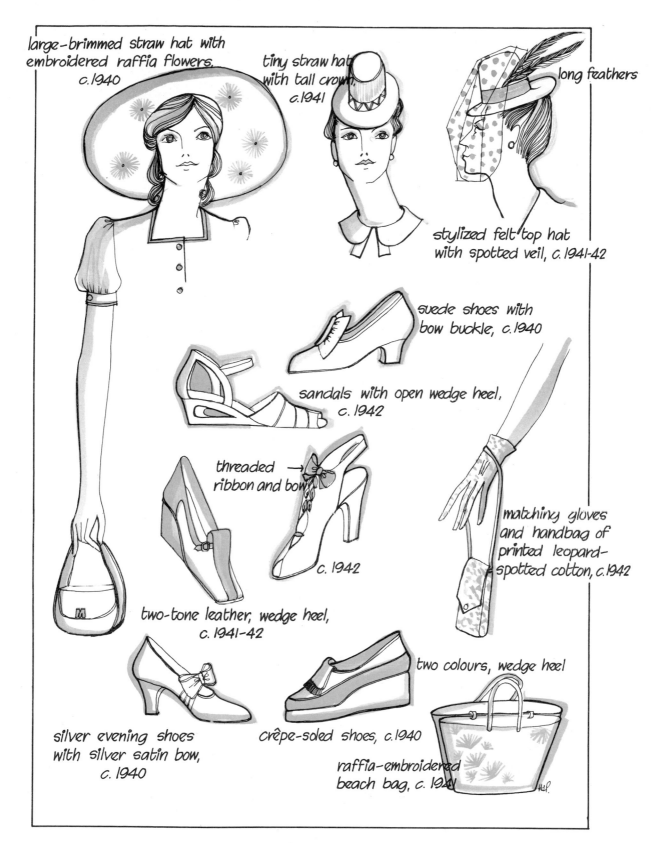

large-brimmed straw hat with embroidered raffia flowers. c.1940

tiny straw hat with tall crown, c.1941

long feathers

stylized felt top hat with spotted veil, c.1941-42

suede shoes with bow buckle, c.1940

sandals with open wedge heel, c.1942

threaded ribbon and bow

c.1942

matching gloves and handbag of printed leopard-spotted cotton, c.1942

two-tone leather, wedge heel, c.1941-42

two colours, wedge heel

silver evening shoes with silver satin bow, c.1940

crêpe-soled shoes, c.1940

raffia-embroidered beach bag, c.1941

pillbox hat with turn-back brim, c. 1943

wool band over ears, tied under chin

knitted hat mounted on turban, c. 1943·44

breton hat with bow trim, c. 1943

braid trim

straw hat with upturned brim, c. 1944

braid bow

fine veil, lace edge

straw hat, wide brim and tall crown, c. 1944

gold lace snood with purple velvet trimming, c. 1943-44

ceramic clips, c. 1944

suede shoes with side lacing and thick crêpe soles, c. 1943

suede shoes with loop and tongue of leather, c. 1943

soft leather gloves with buttoned cuff, c. 1943-44

shoes with high wedge heels, inset contrast bands, c. 1944

c. 1943

suede shoes with high stand buckle

# ACCESSORIES c. 1945·46

fine straw hat with wide flat
brim, round shallow crown, c.1945

three velvet ribbons

domed velvet skull-cap,
c.1945-46

small breton hat on
stiffened headband, c.1946

small thick round
crownless hat with
chiffon veil, c.1945

short suede boot with
a double platform sole, c.1945

bead chain with
threaded pendant,
c.1945

walking shoes, c.1945

crocheted cotton gloves,
c.1945-46

long suede gloves with
punched decoration, c.1945

buckle trim

wooden rings

red, white and blue knitted
beach bag, c.1945-46

darts

suede and leather court shoes,
c.1946

double beach bag of
soft linen, c.1945

fine straw hat trimmed with an ostrich feather and flowers, c.1947

high-heeled sling-back shoes with top-stitching and wrapover button detail, c. 1947

fine platform sole

high-heeled suede sandals, c. 1947-48

large two-tone beret, bow trimming, c. 1949

two-tone court shoes with peep toes, c. 1948-49

fur trim

C/F zip

punched hole decoration

zip fastening

navy blue and cream suede boots with high heels, c. 1948

large soft beret with decorative hatpin, c. 1948

long leather boots with side zip fastening and fur trim, c. 1949

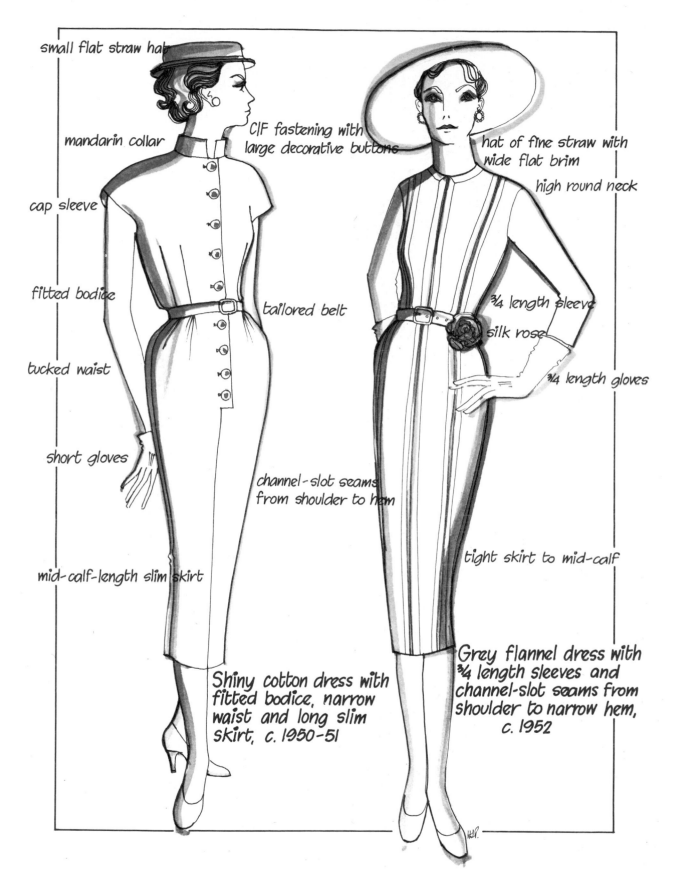

small flat straw hat

mandarin collar

cap sleeve

fitted bodice

tucked waist

short gloves

mid-calf-length slim skirt

C/F fastening with large decorative buttons

tailored belt

channel-slot seams from shoulder to hem

hat of fine straw with wide flat brim

high round neck

¾ length sleeve

silk rose

¾ length gloves

tight skirt to mid-calf

Shiny cotton dress with fitted bodice, narrow waist and long slim skirt, c. 1950-51

Grey flannel dress with ¾ length sleeves and channel-slot seams from shoulder to narrow hem, c. 1952

# DAY DRESSES c. 1953·54

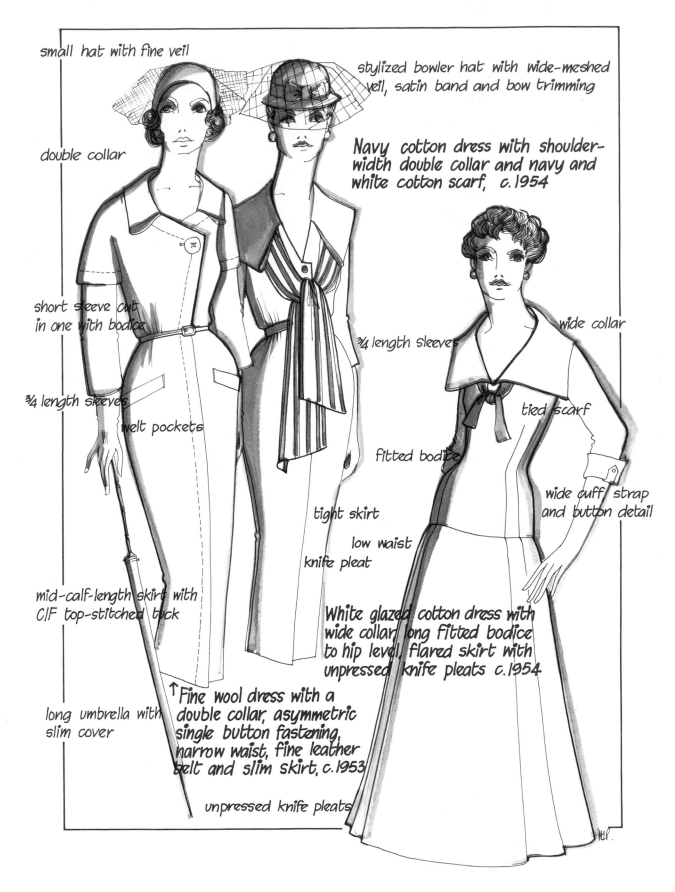

small hat with fine veil

stylized bowler hat with wide-meshed veil, satin band and bow trimming

double collar

Navy cotton dress with shoulder-width double collar and navy and white cotton scarf, c. 1954

short sleeve cut in one with bodice

¾ length sleeves

wide collar

¾ length sleeves

tied scarf

welt pockets

fitted bodice

wide cuff strap and button detail

tight skirt

low waist

knife pleat

mid-calf-length skirt with CIF top-stitched tuck

White glazed cotton dress with wide collar, long fitted bodice to hip level, flared skirt with unpressed knife pleats c. 1954

long umbrella with slim cover

↑Fine wool dress with a double collar, asymmetric single button fastening, narrow waist, fine leather belt and slim skirt, c. 1953

unpressed knife pleats

small felt hat, rose trim

low bound square neckline

cap sleeve

collar and front bodice panel cut in one piece

'U' shaped neck

long fitted bodice to low hipline

fitted bodice

short sleeves

hip seam

flat bow decoration

low waist

double box pleats

gathered skirt

below knee length

Cotton dress with cape collar cut in one with the fitted bodice, low hip seam, full skirt, c.1955

gathered skirt

Pink cotton dress with grey cotton binding on square neckline matching bows and belt at hip. c.1955

Orange wool crêpe dress with short sleeves, fitted bodice, low waist detail, full skirt, c.1956

high slim heels, pointed toes

# DAY DRESSES c. 1957·60

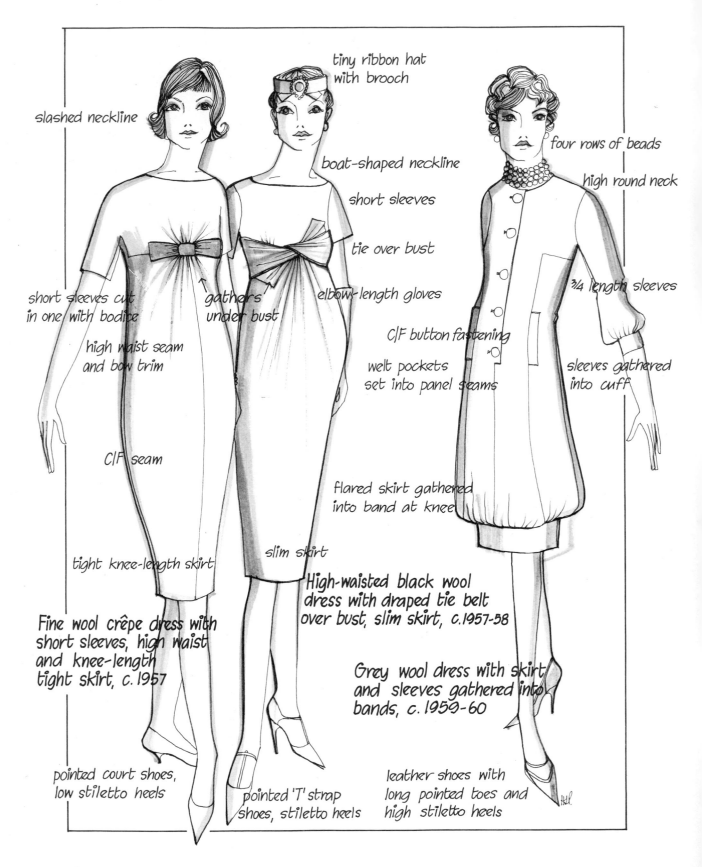

slashed neckline

tiny ribbon hat with brooch

boat-shaped neckline

short sleeves

tie over bust

four rows of beads

high round neck

short sleeves cut in one with bodice

gathers under bust

elbow-length gloves

¾ length sleeves

high waist seam and bow trim

C/F button fastening

welt pockets set into panel seams

sleeves gathered into cuff

C/F seam

flared skirt gathered into band at knee

tight knee-length skirt

slim skirt

High-waisted black wool dress with draped tie belt over bust, slim skirt, c.1957-58

Fine wool crêpe dress with short sleeves, high waist and knee-length tight skirt, c. 1957

Grey wool dress with skirt and sleeves gathered into bands, c. 1959-60

pointed court shoes, low stiletto heels

pointed 'T' strap shoes, stiletto heels

leather shoes with long pointed toes and high stiletto heels

Strapless cotton bra with fine lace edging, lightweight boning, c.1950

elasticated panel

Lace bra, finely wired cups, c.1951

Strapless wired bra of spotted cotton trimmed with fine lace, c.1952

Long-line corset with zip fastening, pointed hem, ribbon frill and suspenders, c.1951-52

ribbon frill, long ribbon suspenders

High-waisted corset with elasticated panels and suspenders, gathered sides, c.1950-51

Short lace and elasticated cotton corset, c.1951-52

lace frill, bow trim

fine lace edging

shaped seams

high hip level

Strapless lace-edged brocade long-line corset with low waist, c.1952

Elasticated strapless bra with fine lace frill, light boning, c.1951

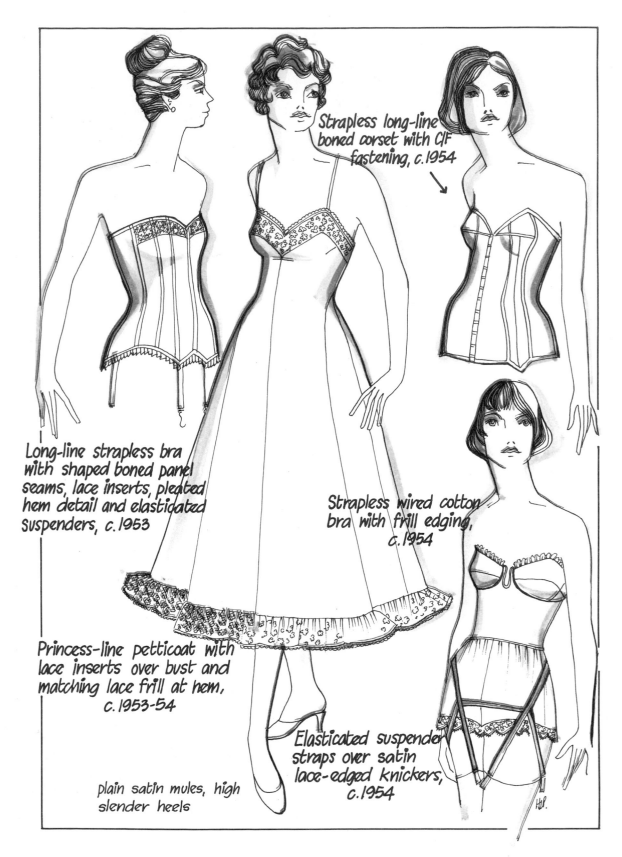

Strapless long-line boned corset with C/F fastening, c.1954

Long-line strapless bra with shaped boned panel seams, lace inserts, pleated hem detail and elasticated suspenders, c.1953

Strapless wired cotton bra with frill edging, c.1954

Princess-line petticoat with lace inserts over bust and matching lace frill at hem, c.1953-54

Elasticated suspender straps over satin lace-edged knickers, c.1954

plain satin mules, high slender heels

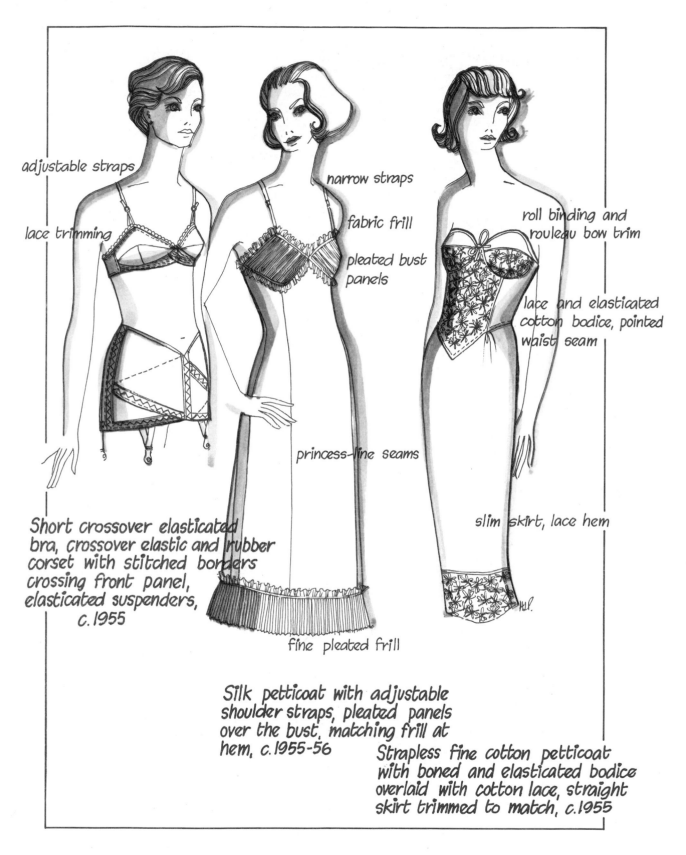

adjustable straps

lace trimming

narrow straps

fabric frill

pleated bust panels

roll binding and rouleau bow trim

lace and elasticated cotton bodice, pointed waist seam

princess-line seams

slim skirt, lace hem

Short crossover elasticated bra, crossover elastic and rubber corset with stitched borders crossing front panel, elasticated suspenders, c.1955

fine pleated frill

Silk petticoat with adjustable shoulder straps, pleated panels over the bust, matching frill at hem, c.1955-56

Strapless fine cotton petticoat with boned and elasticated bodice overlaid with cotton lace, straight skirt trimmed to match, c.1955

narrow adjustable
shoulder straps

wide half-straps
cut in one with
the bra cups

high waistline

elasticated side
panels

adjustable elasticated
suspenders

deep 'V' shaped scoop

C/B fastening

circular-stitched
bra cups

light boning

Waist-length strapless bra with
low scooped back and light
boning, c.1959-60

Long-line lace and elasticated
cotton bra, high-waisted rubber
and elastic corset with side
zip fastening, c.1957

lace trimming

separated bra cups

C/F fastening

elasticated side panels

fine cording and boning

lace trimming

Combined bra and corset
of cotton brocade with wide
elasticated side panels, light
boning on C/F 'V' shaped panel
and on side panels, c.1959-60

long ribbon suspenders with
buckle adjustments

104

wide halter straps

inset contrast-fabric band

bikini top

hip-length skirt with inset band on hem

halter rouleau straps tied at the back of the neck

low 'V' shaped neckline

narrow rouleau belt, bow tie

glass bead bracelet

tight knee-length trousers

three-button fastening at knee

Bright yellow cotton beach top and slim-fitting trousers with button detail at the knee, c.1951-52

leather sandals

Bikini and short skirt in brightly coloured cotton print, c.1950

flat soft leather shoes, gathered instep detail

large fine straw hat

high round neck with shirt collar

extended shoulder line

strapless top with turn-down cuff

D/B fastening

bare midriff

D/B waistband

low square neckline

braid trim

extended shoulder

turnups

tight-fitting knee-length trousers

fitted bodice

shaped waist seam

**Dual-fabric suntop and short shorts with cuff and turnups in alternating fabrics, c.1954**

**Tennis dress with low square neckline, fitted bodice, flared skirt with inverted box pleats, c.1953-54**

inverted box pleat

short skirt, braid trim

flat-heeled leather shoes, bow trim

**Short D/B cotton jacket with cap sleeves, tight knee-length trousers with D/B waistband, c.1953**

narrow collar and revers

stitched mandarin collar

cut-away armholes

decorative braid fastening

S/B fastening

¾ length flared sleeves

fitted bodice

deep waistband

decorative stitching

knife-pleated skirt

Tennis dress with halter neckline, mock collar and revers, S/B button fastening and knife-pleated skirt, c.1955-56

narrow fitted trousers

strapless draped bustline

fitted seamed bodice

gathered side panels, piped inserts and rouleau bow decoration

stitched hem

opening

Red satin suit with black braid loop fastenings and black top-stitching on collar, sleeves and trouser hems, c.1954

Bathing costume with draped bustline, seamed and boned tight-fitting bodice, gathered side panels, c. 1955-56

straight neckline, bound edge

bow ties

fine straw hat with down-turned brim

roll-bound keyhole neckline, rouleau bow tie fastening

cap sleeves

wide flared bodice

long tubular bodice

bow trim

low bound waistline

large patch pockets

large cloche beach hat, wide threaded band

Sage green tent-shaped towelling beach top, c. 1958-59

two-tier skirt

bound hems

knee length

wide shoulder straps

stiffened bra

Navy blue and white cotton bikini, c. 1960

low stiletto heels

Sundress with long tubular bodice to hipline, neck, waist and hems of tiered skirt bound in contrast fabric, bow trim, c. 1957-58

brief bikini knickers

narrow pointed toes

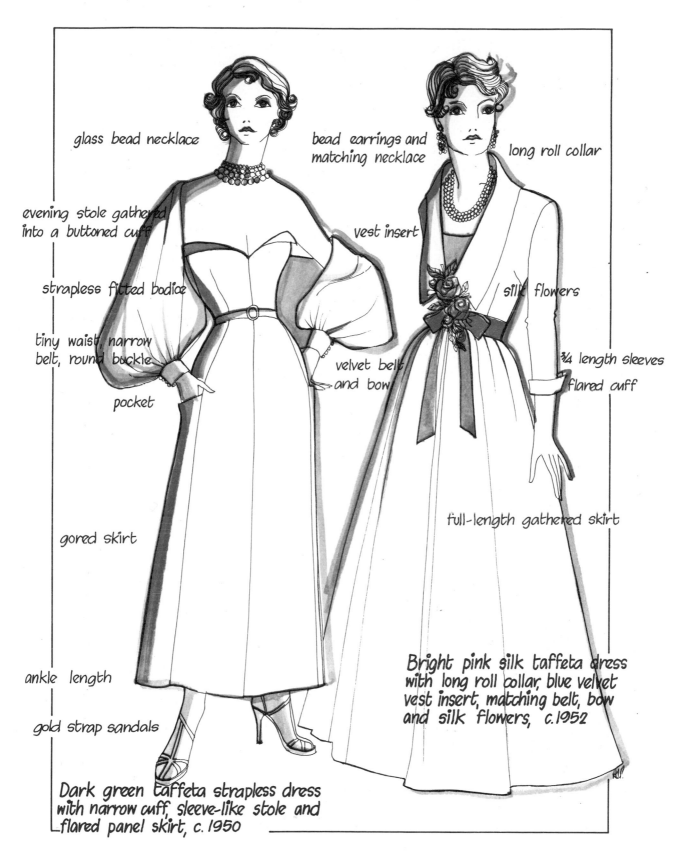

glass bead necklace

bead earrings and
matching necklace

long roll collar

evening stole gathered
into a buttoned cuff

vest insert

strapless fitted bodice

silk flowers

tiny waist, narrow
belt, round buckle

velvet belt
and bow

¾ length sleeves

flared cuff

pocket

gored skirt

full-length gathered skirt

ankle length

gold strap sandals

Bright pink silk taffeta dress
with long roll collar, blue velvet
vest insert, matching belt, bow
and silk flowers, c.1952

Dark green taffeta strapless dress
with narrow cuff, sleeve-like stole and
flared panel skirt, c.1950

bead and chain hairband

bead necklace and matching earrings

double rouleau straps

wide straps

bead and chain necklace

strapless draped bodice

bow detail

straight → neckline

bow trim

narrow waist

C/F seam

asymmetric draped side panel

gathered hip detail

long gloves

large taffeta bow

Strapless draped chiffon evening dress, c. 1953

Wild silk dress with high straight neckline, long fitted bodice, large contrast taffeta bow on side, unpressed inverted box pleat, c. 1954

Ankle-length mauve taffeta evening dress, tight-fitting to hip, with bow-shaped bra-bodice, flared skirt with gathered side panels, c. 1953

strapless neckline

lace band and bow with trailing ends

fitted bodice

¾ length gloves

full gathered overskirt

unpressed hem

ankle-length underskirt

lace shoes

high slim heels, pointed toes

Pink silk taffeta strapless dress trimmed with grey lace, c.1955

round shoulder clips

deep 'V' shaped neckline

high draped belt

horizontal draped hip basque

full gathered skirt

Smoke-grey silk chiffon dress with draped bodice and full gathered skirt from hipline, c.1956

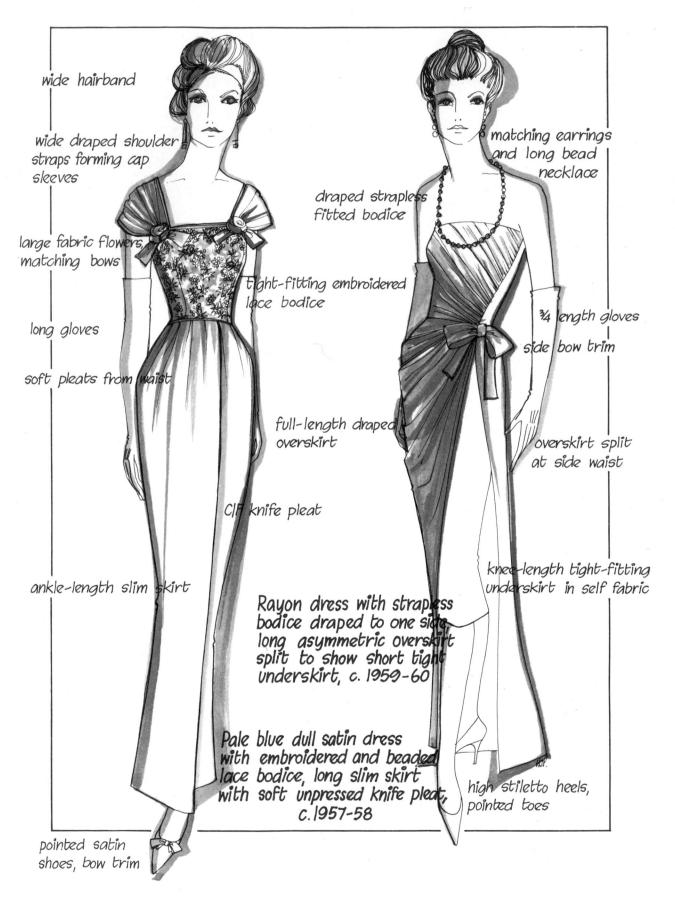

wide hairband

wide draped shoulder
straps forming cap
sleeves

large fabric flowers,
matching bows

long gloves

soft pleats from waist

ankle-length slim skirt

matching earrings
and long bead
necklace

draped strapless
fitted bodice

tight-fitting embroidered
lace bodice

¾ length gloves

side bow trim

full-length draped
overskirt

overskirt split
at side waist

C|F knife pleat

knee-length tight-fitting
underskirt in self fabric

Rayon dress with strapless
bodice draped to one side,
long asymmetric overskirt
split to show short tight
underskirt, c. 1959-60

Pale blue dull satin dress
with embroidered and beaded
lace bodice, long slim skirt
with soft unpressed knife pleat,
c. 1957-58

pointed satin
shoes, bow trim

high stiletto heels,
pointed toes

# WEDDING DRESSES c.1950·52

beaded pillbox hat

two-tier short veil edged with tiny pearls

wide roll collar

beaded and embroidered waistcoat-bodice

long tight sleeves

C/F button fastening

side-gathered skirt

Wedding dress with embroidered and beaded waistcoat-bodice, flared skirt with gathered side panels, slight train, c.1950

small heart-shaped headband, short veil

sweetheart neckline

draped bodice

mock D/B fastening

narrow waist

long tight sleeves, tiny button trim

full gathered skirt

Fine silk dress with fitted bodice, draped bust-line, full skirt gathered from narrow waist, c.1951–52

# WEDDING DRESSES c. 1953·54

headdress of tiny flowers

chiffon veil

flowers

hip-length chiffon veil

shirt-type collar

loop and button

wing collar

C/F button fastening

sleeve cut in one with bodice

gathers →

bust-length bolero

bow-shaped cummerbund

narrow waist

tiny cuff

graduated ribbon trim →

Pale blue-grey satin wedding dress with tight-fitting bodice, C/F button fastening, skirt cut with wide box pleat forming ribbon-decorated centre panel, c.1953

Dull cream satin dress with matching bolero-type jacket to just below bustline, narrow waist, princess-line panels flaring to wide hem, c.1954

# WEDDING DRESSES c.1955·56

circle of flowers with short silk organza veil

small half-hat with long chiffon veil

wide stand collar

vest insert

embroidered and beaded 'U' shaped neckline

soft bow tie

short sleeves

¾ length sleeves

fitted bodice to hip length

embroidered and beaded cuffs and belt at high waist

gathered skirt

ankle length

high slim heels

High-waisted satin dress with embroidered and beaded trimming, flared skirt to floor, c.1956

**Ankle-length cotton dress with wide stand collar, large bow tie, slim bodice, gathered skirt from hipline, c.1955**

# WEDDING DRESSES c.1957·60

tiny beaded pillbox hat

full-length tulle veil

stiffened ribbon headdress

fine full-length veil

high round neckline

embroidered beaded and sequined top

high wide mandarin collar

covered button trim

short bell-shaped sleeve

high waist

tight bodice

¾ length gloves

flared skirt with two unpressed pleats each side of C/F

flat front, full gathers from side waist forming long train at back

Silk satin wedding dress with heavily beaded sequined and embroidered top, matching long tight sleeves, high-waisted skirt, c.1957-58

Watered silk dress with fitted bodice, short bell-shaped sleeves, high mandarin-type collar, skirt with gathered train, c.1959-60

# SUITS c.1950·52

cloche-type hat, wide ribbon band, bow and flower trimming

soft beret

mandarin collar

concealed opening

stand shirt collar

strap opening

buttoned welt pocket

wide batwing sleeve

wide tailored belt

¾ length sleeves cut in one with bodice

patch pockets

long semi-fitted jacket

turn-back cuff

turn-back cuff

hip-length jacket

short gloves

knife-pleated skirt

slim skirt

Grey wool suit with large sleeves gathered into cuffs, narrow waist and tight skirt, c. 1950-51

Knitted wool suit with hip-length semi-fitted jacket, knife-pleated skirt, c. 1952

leather shoes with high slim heels and almond-shaped toes

court shoes with elongated toes and high slender heels

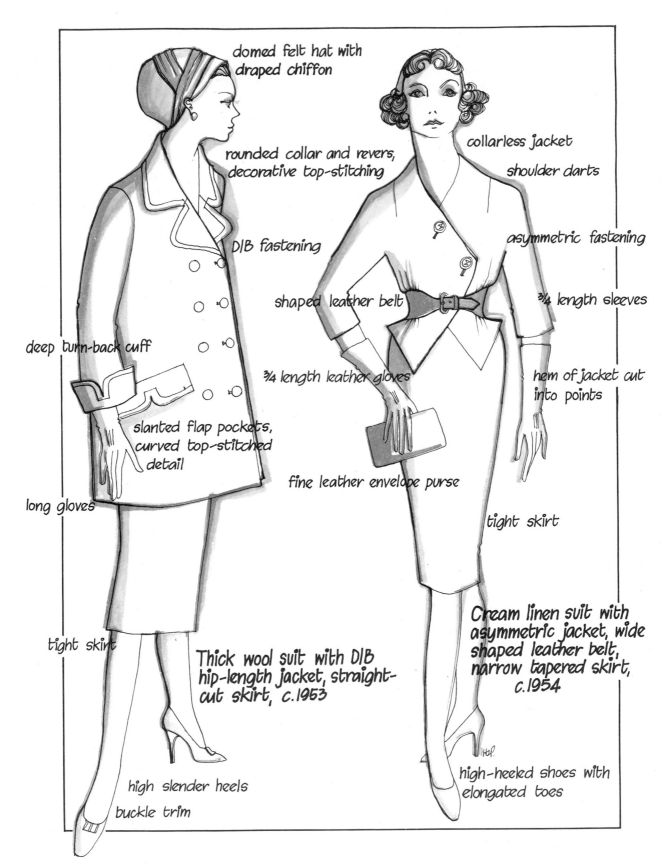

domed felt hat with draped chiffon

collarless jacket

shoulder darts

rounded collar and revers, decorative top-stitching

asymmetric fastening

D/B fastening

¾ length sleeves

shaped leather belt

deep turn-back cuff

hem of jacket cut into points

¾ length leather gloves

slanted flap pockets, curved top-stitched detail

fine leather envelope purse

long gloves

tight skirt

tight skirt

Thick wool suit with D/B hip-length jacket, straight-cut skirt, c.1953

Cream linen suit with asymmetric jacket, wide shaped leather belt, narrow tapered skirt, c.1954

high slender heels

high-heeled shoes with elongated toes

buckle trim

# SUITS c. 1955·56

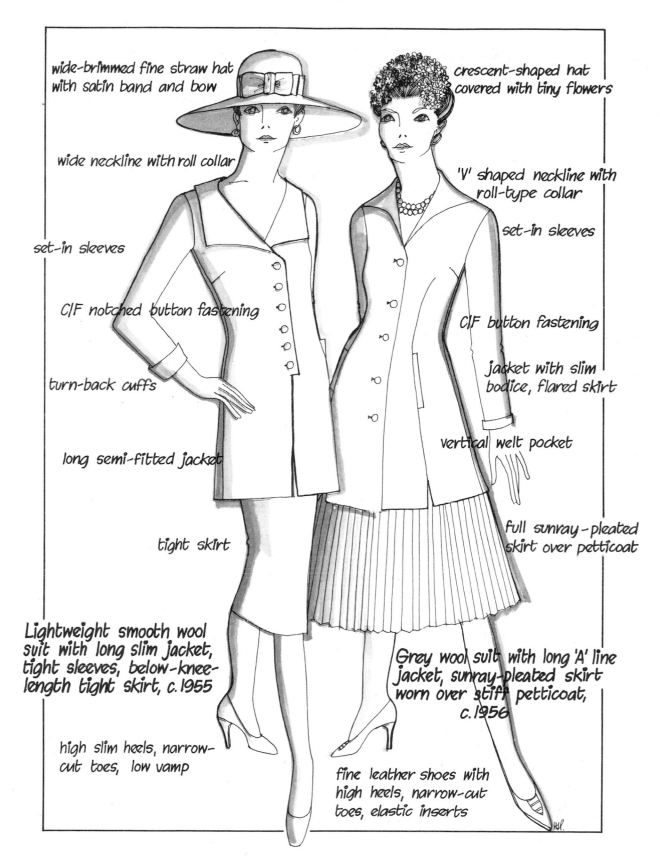

wide-brimmed fine straw hat with satin band and bow

crescent-shaped hat covered with tiny flowers

wide neckline with roll collar

'V' shaped neckline with roll-type collar

set-in sleeves

set-in sleeves

C/F notched button fastening

C/F button fastening

turn-back cuffs

jacket with slim bodice, flared skirt

long semi-fitted jacket

vertical welt pocket

tight skirt

full sunray-pleated skirt over petticoat

Lightweight smooth wool suit with long slim jacket, tight sleeves, below-knee-length tight skirt, c.1955

Grey wool suit with long 'A' line jacket, sunray-pleated skirt worn over stiff petticoat, c.1956

high slim heels, narrow-cut toes, low vamp

fine leather shoes with high heels, narrow-cut toes, elastic inserts

# SUITS c. 1957 · 60

large domed felt hat trimmed with roses

lampshade hat

hairband

wide neckline with D/B braided collar and revers

wide boat-shaped neckline, stand collar

low round neck

bow tie

four-button fastening

short jacket

welt pockets

short jacket

¾ length set-in sleeves

wide belt

rouleau tie belt

¾ length gloves

¾ length sleeves

hip-length jacket

narrow bell-shaped skirt to below knee length

bell-shaped skirt

straight skirt

Orange wool hopsack suit with short D/B braided jacket, narrow bell-shaped skirt with soft waist tucks, c.1957-58

Blue-grey fine wool suit with D/B semi-fitted jacket, four self-covered buttons, knee-length straight skirt, c.1960

Blue linen suit with short jacket and narrow bell-shaped skirt, c.1958

high fine stiletto heels, pointed toes and narrow strap

# COATS c. 1950·52

velvet pillbox hat, brooch trimming

draped hat, large feather trimming

collar set into darts

contrast stand collar

wide contrast revers

large buttons

three-button fastening

sleeves cut in one with the bodice

waist darts

flared sleeves

full skirt

edge-to-edge front

deep cuff

mid-calf length

Flared edge-to-edge coat with contrast stand collar, revers to hem and deep cuffs, c. 1951-52

Velvet coat with large collar, fitted bodice, narrow waist, s/B fastening, covered buttons and mid-calf-length skirt, c. 1950-51

court shoes with high slender heels

# COATS c.1953·54

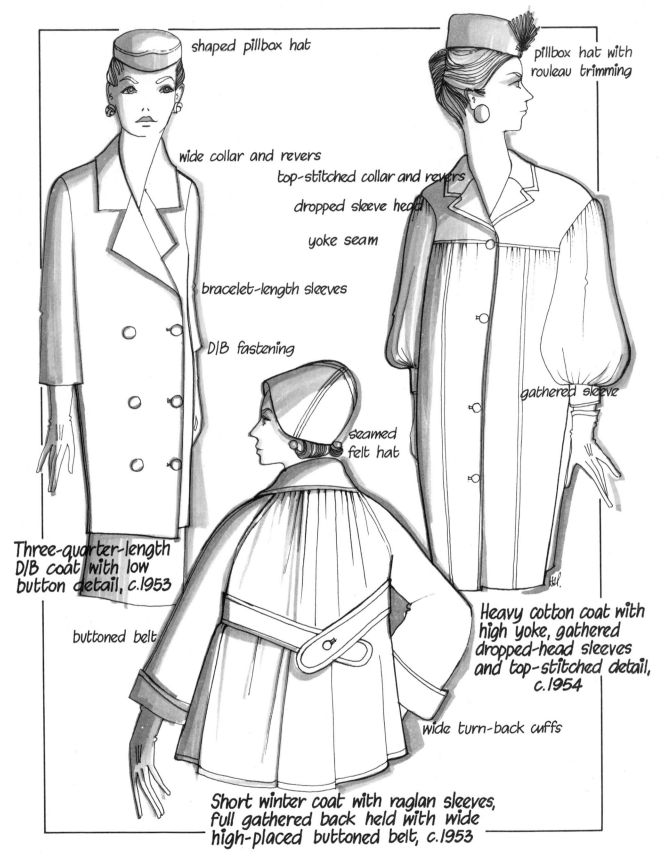

shaped pillbox hat

pillbox hat with rouleau trimming

wide collar and revers

top-stitched collar and revers

dropped sleeve head

yoke seam

bracelet-length sleeves

D/B fastening

seamed felt hat

gathered sleeve

**Three-quarter-length D/B coat with low button detail, c.1953**

buttoned belt

**Heavy cotton coat with high yoke, gathered dropped-head sleeves and top-stitched detail, c.1954**

wide turn-back cuffs

**Short winter coat with raglan sleeves, full gathered back held with wide high-placed buttoned belt, c.1953**

# COATS c. 1955 · 56

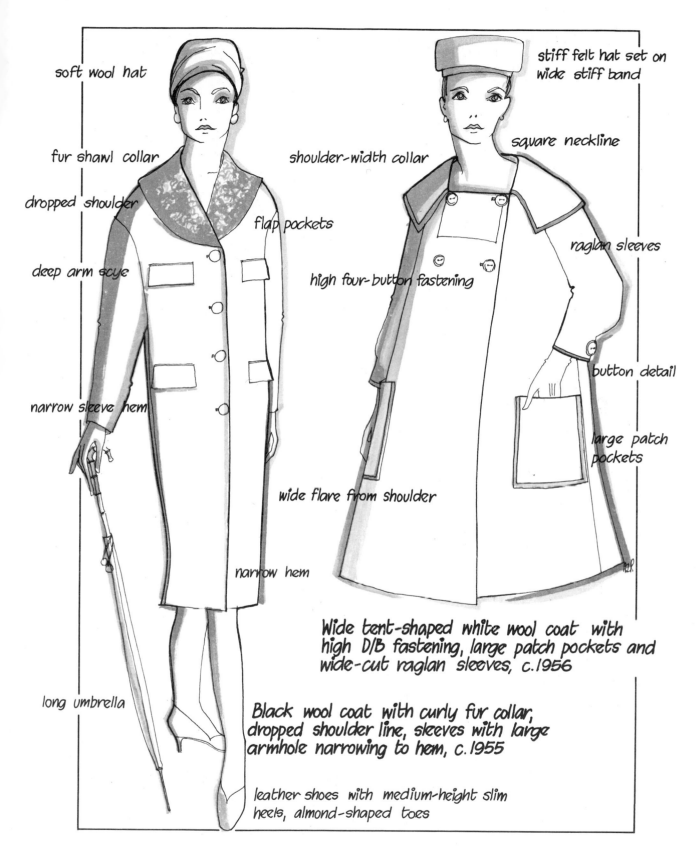

soft wool hat

fur shawl collar

dropped shoulder

deep arm scye

narrow sleeve hem

long umbrella

shoulder-width collar

flap pockets

high four-button fastening

narrow hem

wide flare from shoulder

stiff felt hat set on wide stiff band

square neckline

raglan sleeves

button detail

large patch pockets

Wide tent-shaped white wool coat with high D/B fastening, large patch pockets and wide-cut raglan sleeves, c.1956

Black wool coat with curly fur collar, dropped shoulder line, sleeves with large armhole narrowing to hem, c.1955

leather shoes with medium-height slim heels, almond-shaped toes

pillbox hat

soft felt hat, velvet ribbon trim

tie neckline

brooch

wide fringed cape collar

high D/B fastening

gathers

slim set-in sleeves

four flap pockets

flared sleeve with fringed detail

S/B cream linen coat with top-stitching on C/F and on decorative flap pockets, c.1957-59

wide hemline

Heavy wool D/B winter coat with large fringed cape collar and matching sleeve trim, c.1960

pointed shoes, strap detail

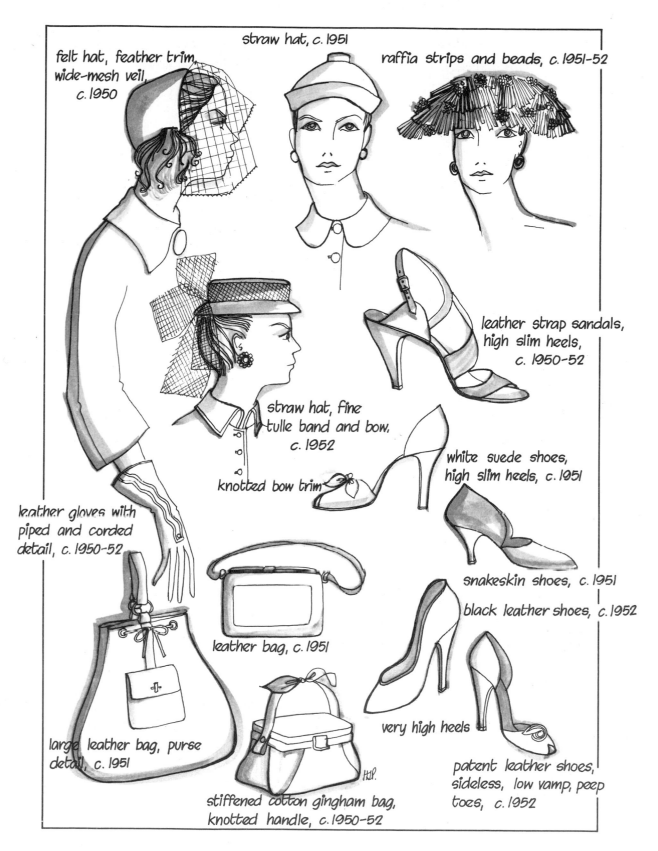

straw hat, c. 1951

felt hat, feather trim,
wide-mesh veil,
c. 1950

raffia strips and beads, c. 1951-52

leather strap sandals,
high slim heels,
c. 1950-52

straw hat, fine
tulle band and bow,
c. 1952

knotted bow trim

white suede shoes,
high slim heels, c. 1951

leather gloves with
piped and corded
detail, c. 1950-52

snakeskin shoes, c. 1951

black leather shoes, c. 1952

leather bag, c. 1951

very high heels

large leather bag, purse
detail, c. 1951

stiffened cotton gingham bag,
knotted handle, c. 1950-52

patent leather shoes,
sideless, low vamp, peep
toes, c. 1952

soft felt hat with shaped brim, c. 1953

wired hat in spotted cotton with ribbon-bound edge, c. 1953

plastic beads, c. 1953-54

stylized beret, bow trim, c. 1954

soft wool hat with side flaps, rouleau trim, c. 1954

nylon gloves, frilled cuff, c. 1954

plastic necklace, c. 1953-54

gold kid strap sandals, c. 1954

long evening gloves, c. 1953-54

soft leather handbag, wide flat handle, c. 1953

crocodile handbag, c. 1953-54

suede and leather two-tone shoes, button detail, c. 1954

silver kid shoes with crystal bead edging, rouleau strap, c. 1953

leather shoes with contrast heel strip and toecap, c. 1954

satin evening shoes, rouleau bow trimming, c. 1953

# ACCESSORIES c.1955·56

bow-trimmed felt hat, narrow brim, c.1955

draped breton-type hat, silk rose trim, c.1956

straw breton with fabric band trim, c.1956

hat with gathered crown, deep back brim, c.1956

leather shoulder bag, c.1955

plastic bucket-bag, buckled strap handle, c.1955-56

leather shoes, cut-out detail, c.1956

leather bag, metal handle, c.1955-56

leather shoes with squat heels, threaded bow decoration, c.1955-56

short boots, high heels, side zip fastening, bow trim, c.1955

soft leather bag, c.1955

low slim heels, pointed toes, punched hole decoration, c.1956

two-tone shoes with buckled strap, c.1956

# ACCESSORIES c.1957·60

pointed toes, laced detail, c.1957-58

two-tone leather

high stiletto heels, narrow pointed toes, c.1959-60

high stiletto heels, c.1959

c.1958-59

pointed toes, rouleau bow detail, c.1957-58

high stiletto heels, low vamp, narrow pointed toes, c.1960

mock leopardskin hat, c.1958-59

brooch

soft leather bag with two fine handles, c.1959

tall straw hat, shallow brim, large flower, c.1957-58

large plastic handbag, purse detail, top-stitching, c.1959-60

felt hat, 'V' shaped bead trim, c.1958

leather bag, strap and buckle fastening and double handles, c.1960

domed hat covered with silk roses, c.1959